What Happens After the Rapture?

From the Rapture to the Second Coming

by

Al Gist

What Happens After the Rapture? - From the Rapture to the Second Coming

Printed in the U.S.A.

ISBN-13:

978-1514823385

ISBN-10:

1514823381

Unless otherwise indicated, Bible quotations are taken from The King James Version.

www.maranathaevangelisticministries.com

email: al_gist@hotmail.com

Table of Contents

Introduction.. 4

Lesson 1 - One Second After the Rapture.................. 5
    Lesson 1 Quiz..23

Lesson 2 - Between the Rapture and the Tribulation.....25
    Lesson 2 Quiz..42

Lesson 3 - The First Half of the Tribulation..............44
    Lesson 3 Quiz..67

Lesson 4 - The Middle of the Tribulation..................69
    Lesson 4 Quiz..86

Lesson 5 - The Last Half of the Tribulation...............88
    Lesson 5 Quiz..103

What Happens After the Rapture?

Introduction

God gives us a lot of information in His Word about the events that will happen on earth after the Rapture of the Church. Putting it mildly, it will be a day of unbelievable chaos, confusion, bloodshed, crime, warfare, persecutions of torture and executions, and many cataclysmic judgments of God. According to what Jesus told us in His Olivet Discourse, it will be the absolute worst time in all of human history (Matt. 24:21) to be alive on planet earth and if Christ did not return to destroy the enemies of God in the end, evil men would annihilate the human race altogether (Matt. 24:22). No words can adequately describe the horror of that coming time. It will be "Hell on Earth"!

But, the good news today is that no one has to go through that seven years of Tribulation. God, in His great mercy, has provided a **way** for each of us living in the Church Age to escape this earth BEFORE the Tribulation begins. And that **way** is through **The Way**, Jesus Christ (John 14:6).

For Christians, this study will help us to know WHAT WE'RE GOING TO MISS on earth, after the Rapture. For those who are NOT Christian, I pray that it will awaken them to their immediate need of finding salvation in Jesus Christ.

"What Happens After the Rapture" is an eye-opening study of the events that will happen on earth after the Rapture until the time of our Lord's glorious Second Coming. It does not cover the heavenly events of the Church during that time. Also, because this study is designed to use in a group study, in five lessons, time and space constraints do not allow for every detail to be discussed. We could easily double or triple the size of these five lessons with all the information God gives us on this topic in His Word.

So, prepare yourself for an AWAKENING as we explore the Scriptures to determine "What Happens After the Rapture".

What Happens After the Rapture?

Lesson 1
One Second After the Rapture

1 Thess. 4:16 - For the Lord Himself shall descend from heaven with a shout, with the voice of the archangel, and with the trump of God: and the dead in Christ shall rise first:

17   Then we which are alive and remain shall be caught up together with them in the clouds, to meet the Lord in the air: and so shall we ever be with the Lord.

18   Wherefore, comfort one another with these words.

5:3 - For when they shall say, Peace and safety; then sudden destruction cometh upon them, as travail upon a woman with child; and they shall not escape.

I want to talk about this last verse first…
This verse is often used to describe the scene after the Lord's Second Coming when Jesus will burst upon the inhabitants of this world with great wrath and power. And with fire flashing in His eyes, He will destroy God's enemies with the Sword of His mouth. There's no doubt that that is going to be a day of great bloodshed and destruction.

But, once again, we see the error of getting the Rapture mixed up with the Second Coming because Paul is NOT talking about the Second Coming here! How do we know this?
Let me give you TWO good reasons:

1. CONTEXT

In the previous chapter, Paul had just talked about the event of the
Rapture! In fact, most would agree that 1 Thess. 4:13-17 is the one
passage in the NT that gives us the most details about the Rapture. And
it concludes with…

1 Thess. 4:18 - Wherefore comfort one another with these words.

And certainly, **for a Christian**, the thought of the Rapture is extremely
comforting… knowing that we will be going to be with our Lord Jesus
and also joining all of our Christian loved ones who have gone on
before us.

What a day that will be! So, "…comfort **one another** [other
CHRISTIANS] with these words".

But listen to me….
There is _nothing_ comforting about the Rapture for the unsaved!

So then, immediately after talking about the Rapture in chapter 4, Paul
continues in chapter 5 talking about why it's unnecessary for him to say
anything about the TIMING of the Rapture (We'll talk more about that
in a minute.)

And then, in verse 3, when he says that people will be saying "Peace
and safety", he is STILL talking about the time of the Rapture. And
even AFTER that, in verses 4-8, he goes on to talk about how we
Christians of the Church Age are the "children of light" who should be
watching for "THAT DAY" and it should NOT come upon US
unexpectedly like a thief in the night.

Obviously, we Christians are looking for the Rapture, NOT the Second
Coming!
So, CONTEXT says that our Scripture text (vs. 3) is talking about the
days before the Rapture.

The second reason we know that our Scripture text is a reference to the
Rapture is because…

2. Before the Second Coming, no one will be saying "Peace and safety".

We don't have time to go into a lot of detail here, but we will see it in Lesson 5. The Bible clearly teaches that the last half of the Tribulation, leading up to the Lord's Second Coming, will be filled with war and bloodshed all over the planet. It certainly WILL NOT be a time of peace and safety.

But some would argue that they will not be saying, "We finally HAVE peace and safety", but that they will be saying, "Oh! How we NEED peace and safety".

But this doesn't appear to be the case because of what Paul says right after that in the same verse.

Mankind will be saying that we have finally ACHIEVED peace and safety, because **in contrast to that**, Paul says that THEN sudden DESTRUCTION (the very opposite of peace and safety) will come… And that destruction will be so widespread and overwhelming that "…they shall not escape."

The Rapture will mark the END of the day of GRACE and will be the BEGINNING of the time leading into the day of God's wrath… the time of the Tribulation.

Here's the point I'm trying to emphasize…
When most of us think about the Rapture, we think about the great joy and celebration associated with it. And that is absolutely true… **FOR THE CHRISTIANS!** But for the lost people who are left behind, it will be a day of DESTRUCTION!

So, obviously, from this verse, at the very time when everything appears to be going pretty good…
And the idea of any worldwide calamity looks very unlikely…
And everyone is getting comfortable with their peaceable lifestyle…
BOOM!   The Rapture happens!

So, from (1) CONTEXT and (2) WHAT WE KNOW ABOUT THE DAYS OF THE TRIBULATION JUST BEFORE THE SECOND COMING, Paul is telling us that when the **Rapture** happens, it will ***cause*** a day of great calamity and destruction on earth!

Now, to get a picture of that, I want us to think about two things:
(1) What will the Rapture will be like, and
(2)   What will this world be like **after** we Christians are caught away in the Rapture.

To help us develop a kind of mental picture of what this is going to be like, let's do it this way…
If you were going to use **just one word** to describe the Rapture, OR to describe what this world will be like AFTER the Rapture, what word would you use?

Well, let me share just two words that I think accurately describe what the Rapture's going to be like. And then, we'll see if we can come up with a couple of words that describe the scene AFTER the Rapture. Together, I think this will give us a picture of what this world is going to go through at the time of the Rapture.

First, there are two words that the Bible teaches us about the Rapture:

1. **Sudden**
2. **Unexpected**

Unlike the time of our Lord's Second Coming, when He will burst upon the inhabitants of this world riding a great white stallion, with eyes flashing fire and speaking utter destruction upon His enemies with the "sword of His mouth"… a time when Matt. 24:30 says that all the people of the world "shall **see** the Son of Man coming in the clouds of heaven with power and great glory"…
At the Rapture, I believe the lost world will **not see** or hear Him.

Why do I say that? Because the Bible says that He will come **suddenly** and **unexpectedly**, like a "thief in the night". Now, let me show you how that translates into the idea that it will be an INVISIBLE event to the unsaved people in the world.

In 1 Thess. 4:17 where Paul is describing for us the event of the Rapture, he says that after the "dead in Christ" are resurrected… "Then we which are alive and remain shall be *caught up* together with them in clouds, to meet the Lord in the air…"

The very word "Rapture", even though it is not found in our English bibles, comes the Latin Vulgate version of the Bible written in the late fourth century. The words translated as **"caught up"** in our KJV, are translated in the Latin Vulgate with the word "rapturo" and this is where we get our commonly used word to describe this great event… the word "Rapture".

But, more importantly… In the original Greek (the language in which the New Testament was written), **"caught up"** is translated from the Greek word **"harpazo"**, which, according to Strong's means:
1. To seize, carry off by force
2. To snatch out or away [1]

So, the idea of the "harpazo" (or, the Rapture) by its very definition, is that it will be a ***sudden snatching away***.

It won't be a long, drawn out affair. It won't happen over days and weeks, and months so people can think about what is going on and then try to get on board!

No! It will happen so **suddenly** that WHEN it happens, you're either IN it, or you're not. You're either snatched away from this earth suddenly along with millions of others who are prepared for it, or you're left behind. It will be an INSTANTANEOUS separation of the people of this world. One group will be suddenly GONE… and the rest left here to face the worst time in human history.

In fact, it will happen so suddenly, Paul says in 1 Cor. 15:52 that it will be "In a moment, in the twinkling of an eye". We might say, like a snap of your fingers!

Therefore, because of the QUICKNESS of it, people who are NOT taken up won't even see it happen. Their Christian friend will be there with them in one moment... and SUDDENLY [snap!] that friend will be gone.

Then, right after Paul describes the Rapture in 1 Thess. 4, he says in chapter 5,
1.   But of the times and seasons, brethren, ye have no need that I write unto you.
[What "times and seasons"? The times and seasons when the Rapture is going to occur... I don't have to tell you... WHY?]
2.   For yourselves know perfectly that the day of the Lord [beginning with the Rapture] so cometh as a thief in the night.

So, he was saying that he didn't need to tell the people in Thessalonica WHEN it was going to happen because they already knew that it will happen at a moment when it is so **unexpected**, it will be like "a thief in the night". If he could tell them exactly when it was going to happen, it wouldn't be UNEXPECTED like a thief in the night.

In fact, as we've already read in our opening Scripture, it will actually happen in a time when people are saying "Peace and safety". And that's all Paul has to say about the timing of the Rapture.

So, we've established two very good words to describe the Rapture:
    1.   Sudden (like the snap of your fingers)
    2.   Unexpected (People won't even be thinking about it happening.)

Now, let's see if we can come up with a couple of words that describe what it's going to be like immediately AFTER the Rapture.

The Bible is clear that the Rapture is for **all** born-again Christians. If you have repented of yours sins and personally accepted Jesus Christ as your Savior, committing your life to Him and have accepted Him as your Lord and Savior, YOU WILL BE caught away in the Rapture if you're still alive when it happens. Paul made it clear that it will be those who are **"in Christ"** that will be caught away to meet him in the air... both those who are "dead in Christ" (dead Christians) and those who are "alive and remain". Paul uses the personal pronoun "we" to describe this second group because, as a Christian, he fully expected to be alive when Jesus comes for His Church. But, we know that he suffered the death of a martyr and did not live to see the Rapture.

1 Thess. 4:17a - Then WE [Christians] which are alive and remain shall be caught up together with them in the clouds, to meet the Lord in the air;...

Now, let me tell you what he did NOT say.
"Then we which are prayed up..." shall be caught up...
Or, "we which have achieved a certain spiritual maturity..." shall be caught up.

As far as I can tell here, there's only TWO qualifications for **CHRISTIANS** to be included in that group that is "caught up":
   1.   Being ALIVE
   2.   Remaining (still here after "the dead in Christ" rise up)

And, in 1 Cor. 15:51 where he's talking about getting that new glorified body as we're snatched away to meet the Lord in the air, he says, "We shall not all sleep [die], but we shall **ALL** be changed." So, if you're a true born again believer in Jesus Christ and you're alive when the Rapture happens, you WILL BE included in the Rapture! You will be changed to that new glorified body in a moment, in the twinkling of an eye, and snatched away to meet Jesus in the air!

Now, I know that there are some who teach that if you are not "prayed up" and really living a spirit-filled life (even though you're a Christian) that you'll be left behind to face the horrors of the Tribulation. But Paul said "we shall **ALL** be changed".

So, why am I making such a strong point that ALL believers will be included in the Rapture? Because think about this…

One second after the Rapture… one second after every true Christian in the world has been snatched away from this planet… There won't be one, single Christian in the whole world!

Can you even imagine what that's going to be like?

When a person is saved, the indwelling presence of the Holy Spirit moves into him. And as that person allows God's Spirit to work through him, and IN him, he begins to SHINE with the light of God's love. He becomes a source of SPIRITUAL LIGHT in a sinfully dark world.

1 John 1:5 says that "…God is light, and in Him is no darkness at all." So, when God lives in you, YOU become a light as He shines through you.

Jesus said,
"Ye are the light of the world. A city that is set on a hill cannot be hid. Neither do men light a candle, and put it under a bushel, but on a candlestick; and it giveth light unto all that are in the house. Let your light so shine before men, that they may see your good works, and glorify your Father which is in Heaven." (Matt. 5:14-16)

But when the Rapture occurs and suddenly every single source of that spiritual light is snatched away, **this whole planet will be plunged into <u>absolute, total spiritual darkness</u>!**

Have you ever considered what that means? Well, let me explain it this way…

The Bible also speaks of the manifestations of God coming from us as FRUIT. When you possess the Spirit of God, your life begins to produce the FRUIT of His Spirit… the outward manifestations of WHO is living inside of you!

And Paul described the Fruit of the Spirit to the Galatians as being **nine qualities**:

"...love, joy, peace, long-suffering, gentleness, goodness, faith, meekness, temperance: against such there is no law." Even the laws of men do not forbid love, joy, peace, etc.

But here's what I want you to see...
These things can ONLY come from God as He lives in you! Without the indwelling presence of the Holy Spirit in you, you are INCAPABLE of producing the Fruit of the Spirit.

REAL LOVE can ONLY come from God living in a person! The world has a dirty imitation, but it's NOT the real thing! It's a cheap counterfeit of what God gives us.

REAL JOY can ONLY come when God lives in a person! The world can give you temporary happiness, but ONLY God can give you that deep, lasting, inner joy that even the tragedies of life cannot take away from you.

REAL PEACE can ONLY come when God lives in you! The world can deaden your senses with drugs, and cheap sex, and lies, and deception, and depression, but ONLY God can give you PEACE in the midst of life's raging storms... ONLY God can give you peace that "passeth all understanding" (Phil. 4:7).

REAL PATIENCE and a **LONG-SUFFERING** attitude can ONLY come when God lives in you! Without the working of the Holy Spirit in your life, you CANNOT have a patient and forgiving spirit. Your life will be a series of one blow-up after another! Road rage becomes on-the-job rage and home rage and friendly sports competitions become rage when the outcome doesn't go your way. And even though you may be able to restrain your outbursts of rage at times, inwardly your blood boils. And the slightest offence causes it to come bursting out with hateful, bitter words and actions. And a vengeful heart and bitter spirit keeps you in bondage. WHY? Because a true loving and patient spirit can ONLY come from God! God will set you FREE from that rage and replace it with PATIENCE and a LONG-SUFFERING attitude.

REAL GENTLENESS and **GOODNESS** can ONLY come when God lives in you! The world can produce a façade that looks like goodness on the outside (a kind of charity and humanitarian outreach that impresses the spiritually blind) but it's undergirded with a callus harshness on the inside. Even those who appear to be "gentle and good" and seem to get along well with others have most often built walls around their hearts to protect themselves from all the pain that comes from broken relationships… relationships that were built on lust and not love… relationships built on selfishness and not sacrifice. I'm telling you that ONLY God can produce a GENUINE gentleness and goodness in a person that totally supersedes the thin veil of goodness that a non-Christian can muster!

REAL FAITH can ONLY come when that faith is anchored in God! Sure, people can and often DO put their faith in things that are completely void of God and even sometimes are actually ANTI-God (like Islam). But does that faith move mountains and accomplish great things like eternal salvation? NO

MEEKNESS (a humble spirit) is evident in the life of a Spirit-filled Christian. The world produces arrogance, and pride, and an egotistical attitude and knows nothing of what it means to lovingly sacrifice one's self for others.

Godliness promotes **TEMPERANCE** (self-control). But the world encourages self-indulgence.

Today we live in a society that is progressively moving towards LESS and LESS self-control. Discipline is becoming a thing of bygone generations. Working hard and sacrificing pleasures today in order to achieve a greater goal later is almost unheard of in this day of immediate gratification. The attitude is "I want it all! And I want it NOW!" And we can add to that… that MOST people today think that they DESERVE it all right now!

But this is nothing new. Modern man is no different from those civilizations of the past who knew not God. Like them, he is motivated by "the lust of the flesh, and the lust of the eyes, the pride of life" (1 John 2:16). His motto is, "If it feels good to the flesh, do it". And thus, "every imagination of the thoughts of his heart [is] only evil continually" (Gen. 6:5).

So, what am I trying to say with all of this? Here's the point… Spiritual light and/or Spiritual Fruit can ONLY come from the heart of a Spirit-filled Christian.

- In this world of spiritual darkness, it is only <u>God's people</u> who provide the light that points the way to Christ.
- It's only the Spirit-filled Christian that provides the sweet fragrance of spiritual fruit in this world of filth and the stench of sin.
- It is **ONLY** the Spirit of God working in the lives of Spirit-filled Christians that produces REAL love, joy, peace, long-suffering, gentleness, goodness, faith, meekness, and temperance.

So, what's going to happen when suddenly every single Christian possessing these precious qualities is GONE?

The result will be TOTAL spiritual darkness such as it has never been seen in this world!

- Suddenly… no real love! Hatred will be the norm and the masses will cry out for more blood.

- Suddenly… no real joy! Brutality and callous, blood-gushing sadism will become the "entertainment" that the world demands.

- Instead of joy and peace, it will be a dog-eat-dog world of crime, terrorism, and war.

- The light of love-produced gentleness and goodness will be removed and in its place, persecution, torture, and fanatical hatred will flourish.

- The worship of God in spirit and truth will be replaced with religious deception, false prophets, idolatry, and empty ritual that CANNOT give those precious, God-given qualities.

The Bible teaches us in 2 Thess. 2 that the restraining work of the Holy Spirit will be removed when the Church is taken out. Today, The Holy Spirit works through the lives of believers to restrain the tidal wave of sin and evil that threatens to cover the globe.

2 Thess. 2:7 - …only he [Holy Spirit] who now letteth [restrains] will let [restrain], until he be taken out of the way.

This is a little hard to understand because it's not the Holy Spirit Who will be removed (because we know that people will be saved during the Tribulation), but His **restraint** against sin will be removed. It will be as if God will look down on mankind and say, "Ok. You've always rebelled against me. You've always wanted to do things your way, so I'm going to let you do it your way." And, He will step back and allow sin to flourish unfettered.

If you think this world is bad now… you ain't seen nothin' yet!
(And I pray to God that you won't be here to see it when it does happen.)

So, the first word I would use to describe the post-Rapture situation is **"Darkness"**…
SPIRITUAL DARKNESS… *Unprecedented* spiritual darkness.

There's one more word that *really* describes the overwhelming state of affairs just after the Rapture… CHAOS. We don't base this on Scripture, but plain, simple logic makes it obvious.

When untold millions of people suddenly go missing, unprecedented chaos will ensue. People from every walk of life will suddenly disappear and their absence will derail many governments, banks, and industries. Ten of thousands of mortgages, car loans, and other notes will go unpaid causing the housing industry to collapse and banks to close their doors. Public utilities like electricity, water, and garbage collection will stop until the vacant positions left by the raptured Christians can be filled or bypassed. Millions will be frantically searching for missing loved ones, but they will not be found. Tempers will flare. Conflict and confusion will spread rapidly. And CHAOS will skyrocket as people everywhere try to deal with the SUDDEN and UNEXPECTED disappearance of their friends, loved ones, and co-workers.

So, there we have it… four words (not an all inclusive list by any means) that describe the Rapture and its aftermath:

It will come SUDDENLY and catch the world by surprise because they do not EXPECT it to ever really happen… plunging the remaining citizens of this planet into a time of absolute spiritual DARKNESS and CHAOS.

The Rapture will happen on a day like any other.
- You may be traveling to work.
- Or, you may already be in your work place, going through your normal work routine
- Depending on what side of the planet you're on, you might be sleeping.
- TV programs will be filling people's ears with entertainment and Fox News will be reporting various events and situations around the world and giving their own opinions as to what is needed to fix things.
- Maybe it will be on a weekend when people are fishing, golfing, shopping, or going to sporting events… doing all the myriad of things people do to entertain themselves.

And then, SUDDENLY… and completely UNEXPECTEDLY… it happens!

Mr. Jones is talking to his co-worker at the desk next to him. He asks him a question, but gets no response. So, he turns to see an empty chair. His first thought is, "Man! He sure left in a hurry. I didn't even hear him leave! He must have gone to the restroom or something." But then, he notices his co-worker's clothes are on the chair and his shoes and socks are laying on the floor in front of his chair. **Suddenly and completely unexpectedly, his co-worker is GONE!**

Bill is a passenger on an airliner. He rests his head against the headrest of his seat as he feels the acceleration of the giant engines and the sudden smoothness as the plane's wheels lift off the ground. His eyes are closed and he's thinking about what he's going to say in the company meeting he's going to speak in. Suddenly, he feels some turbulence and thinks, "Nothing to worry about. That happens all the time." But then the plane veers sharply to the right and screams are heard in the cabin as people try to lean in the other direction. Something has gone terribly wrong. **Suddenly and completely unexpectedly, the pilot and co-pilot are GONE...** leaving the plane uncontrolled.

Mrs. Smith wakes up when her husband's alarm goes off. She groans and pulls her pillow over head mumbling something about why he always gets up so early just to read his Bible. But the alarm continues to blast away and so she finally makes a wild slap at it, hitting the snooze. That's when she notices that her husband is not in bed. As she looks dreary eyed at the clock, she notices that it is way too early for him to already be at work, so she calls out, "Jim?" No response. She gets out of bed and walks to the bathroom... then to the kitchen and notices that he has not made coffee yet. Calling his name, she walks all over the house and then, she notices it... His car is still in the driveway. **Suddenly and completely unexpectedly (while she was sleeping) her husband is GONE.**

These three and literally millions more like them all over the world are coming the sudden realization that SOMETHING is seriously wrong.

On "Elm Street" in an American suburb, a woman with a dazed look on her face, still her night gown, walks on the sidewalk crying out the names of her husband and children. Another screams hysterically from her front door, that their children have gone missing. But no one even notices them because there are people up and down Elm street and all through the neighborhood coming out of their houses with that same bewildered look on their faces.

In Mr. Jones' office building, pandemonium has already broken out. People everywhere are missing and fellow workers are gathering in the halls asking if anyone has seen so-and-so. The department manager is telling everyone to stay calm, reassuring them that there is a reasonable explanation for all of this. Suddenly, someone yells that everyone should look at the news on the TV and at least two dozen people try to squeeze into the manager's office to look at the only TV on that floor. A late breaking "News Alert" is flashing across the screen when the well-known national news caster breaks in and begins to explain that there is Late Breaking News. Reports from all over the country are coming in that people have suddenly gone missing. At this point, the government is not making any statements about this strange disappearance, but rumors of an alien invasion or some new Weapon of Mass Destruction are flying about the air waves.

Five minutes later, the Governor appears on the local channel and declares a State of Emergency as hundreds of transportation accidents are being reported all over the state… an airliner at the local airport is reported to have crashed just after take-off for no apparent reason, but pilot error seems to be most obvious answer at this time. All public employees, especially the policemen, firemen, and utility workers are directed to report to work at once, as are the medical staff in all area hospitals.

Every hospital and trauma unit in the whole city is being inundated with injured people. Sirens blast as ambulances crowd the emergency room entrances and police cars race to the scene of the closest accident. It is pure chaos and confusion. Everybody has questions, but no one has answers.

Within minutes, communications systems are dead. A call on any phone only yields a recording saying that the circuits are busy... please try you call again later. Some callers curse and throw their cell phone across the room. Other in offices or businesses tap wildly on the phone buttons trying to get a response, but the irritating recording monotonously repeats itself... "I'm sorry. All circuits are busy now. Please try your call again later."

In the downtown area, traffic is jam packed as there are stalled, wrecked, and simply vacant cars blocking all traffic. Horns are blaring... some people are getting out of their cars trying to look up the street to see what the hold-up us. Tempers are flaring as drivers begin to yell at those ahead of them. Police cars can't even get through the mass of idle cars and a motorcycle policeman is slowly making his way along the sidewalk in the direction of what he thinks is the problem. Driving anywhere in the downtown area has suddenly become impossible.

On the outskirts of town, in the lower rent areas, looters are having a holiday. The police department is scattered and doing its best to help where there are people dead or dying. This presents looters with a great opportunity to steal whatever they want, so one is seen throwing a newspaper rack through the display window in the front of an appliance store. Store alarms are piercing the air as looters crawl through the broken window and begin to carry off TVs, computers, cell phones and anything else they can find.

In perhaps the more virulent areas, criminals with pent up anger see an opportunity to do whatever they want to whomever they want. So, gangs start breaking into homes, raping the women and murdering the men. No one is safe as anarchy bursts into reality from the millions of hearts that harbor seeds of hatred, sick fantasies, and rebellion. Like millions of grass seeds bursting into life producing a thick carpet of green, millions of sin-sick humans are releasing their sinful inner feelings into action producing a carpet of red, blood drenched landscape across the country.

All over the city and all across the country, tens of thousands are dying or are dead because drivers of trucks, car, buses, trains, and airplanes suddenly disappeared, leaving their vehicle driverless to crash into the nearest obstacle. Thousands of medical staff in the hospitals are suddenly gone from their post (some even in the middle of surgeries) leaving the facilities understaffed as the massive overload of injured people begins to come in.

Government agencies of every sort are scrambling to re-establish some sense of order. But endless days and nights of crime, death, and mayhem sweep the land until the President declares a state of emergency and announces the implementation of national curfews, giving law officials and Homeland Security the right to shoot first and ask questions later to enforce the new federal, dictatorial law.

Militaries around the world are ordered on HIGH ALERT under the suspicion that an enemy nation has just made some kind of high tech attach. Air Force jets are scrambling. Nuclear submarines are ordered into readiness and are moving near the ocean's surface preparing to blast their deadly payload into action. Never before have all the nations of the world been so close to making simultaneous attacks on those whom they perceive to be their enemies. The world is on the BRINK of annihilation of all land mammals.

What has happened?

When no one was expecting it to happen…
SUDDENLY, the Rapture has happened.

And all the love, joy, peace, long-suffering, gentleness, goodness, etc. that makes people act in a decent and reasonable fashion has instantaneously evaporated, leaving a dog-eat-dog, every man for himself, mentality of hatred.

Such worldwide chaos and confusion will be unprecedented. Never in all of recorded history will there have ever been such anarchy and bloodshed. Words are completely inadequate to describe the awfulness of that day.

Listen to what I'm saying…
You don't want to be here one second AFTER the Rapture!

If you think that you can wait till later to secure your salvation so that you will be included in the Rapture, **you're making a terrible mistake! It will come suddenly and unexpectedly. By the time you realize what has happened, it will be too late to prepare your heart for the Rapture!**

So, do it now!

Be sure of your salvation <u>right now</u>!

Even <u>one second</u> after the Rapture will be too late!

**(1)http://www.blbclassic.org/lang/lexicon/lexicon.cfm?Strongs=G72
6&t=KJV**

One Second After the Rapture

Lesson 1 Quiz

1.   When Paul says in I Thess. 5:3. "For when they shall say, Peace and safety, then sudden destruction cometh upon them…", is he talking about the people before the Rapture, or the people before the Second Coming?

2.   Today, we Christians of the Church Age are looking forward to (1) The Rapture, or (2) The Second Coming as the next great event?

3.   Two words that describe the Rapture are _____ and _____.

4.   The Greek word that's translated in 1 Thess. 4:17 as "caught up" is the word_____.

5.   And it means a _____ snatching away.

6.   When the Rapture occurs, suddenly the whole world is going to be plunged into absolute spiritual _____.

7.   The first three qualities that Paul uses to describe the Fruit of the Spirit is _____, _____, and _____.

8.   T or F   The Bible teaches in 2 Thess. 2:7 that at the time of the Rapture, the Holy Spirit will be removed from the earth.

9.   In addition to spiritual darkness on the earth AFTER the Rapture, there will be widespread _____.

10.   T or F If you are not sure about your salvation, you should wait until AFTER the Rapture and then be saved during the Tribulation.

One Second After the Rapture

Lesson 1 Quiz Answers

1.   The people before the Rapture

2.   (1) The Rapture

3.   Sudden and Unexpected

4.   Harpazo

5.   sudden

6.   darkness

7.   love, joy, peace

8.   False. Only the RESTRAINT of the Holy Spirit will be removed.

9.   Chaos

10.   FALSE! Although people will be saved during the Tribulation, it will be the worst time in all of history for Christians as they are hunted down and killed in unprecedented fashion for their faith.

What Happens After the Rapture?

Lesson 2
Between the Rapture and the Tribulation

Sometimes, people think that the Rapture is the event that starts the seven year Tribulation. But this is not so. The Rapture is the concluding event of the Church Age. It is not the initiating event of the Tribulation.

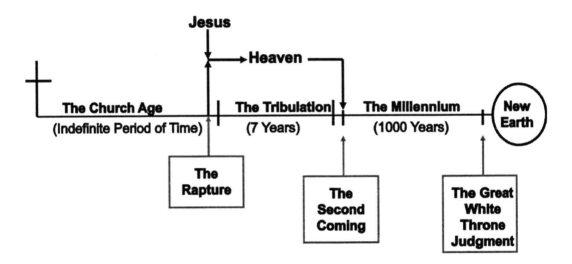

You see, during this Age of Grace that we call the Church Age (in which you and I now live), God has turned His attention to the Gentile nations of the world and is gathering out that very special group of people from among the population of the world that is The Church... or, the Bride of Christ. And, when that last person has been born again into the family of God and the "Bride" is complete, then The Groom (Jesus) will come for His Bride in the Rapture and carry us away to our new home in Heaven. And this will conclude the Church Age.

Then, some time after that, this world will be plunged into the worst time of pain, and heartache, and bloodshed that it has ever experienced. It will be the "Time of Jacob's Trouble" (Jer. 30:7)... "Daniel's Seventieth Week" (Dan. 9:27)... the "Day of Tribulation" (Matt. 24:21). It will consist of seven years of 360 days each for a total of 2520 days in which many things will happen on this planet. We will be looking at those Tribulation events in subsequent lessons.

Well, if the Rapture concludes the Church Age, then what event will initiate the Tribulation? Daniel gives us the answer.

In Daniel 9:24-27, the prophet is told that God intends to deal with his (Daniel's) people (the Jews) for another 70 weeks of years (70 x 7 = 490 years). And then he is told that that 490 years will be divided into three time segments:

$$
\begin{aligned}
7 \text{ weeks of years} &= 7 \times 7 = &49 \text{ years} \\
62 \text{ weeks of years} &= 62 \times 7 = &434 \text{ years} \\
1 \text{ week of years} &= 1 \times 7 = &7 \text{ years} \\
\hline
\text{TOTAL} &= &490 \text{ years}
\end{aligned}
$$

Daniel is told that the 490 years will begin when the decree is given for the Jews to return and rebuild the city of Jerusalem.

Daniel 9:25 - Know therefore and understand, *that* **from the going forth of the commandment to restore and to build Jerusalem** unto the Messiah the Prince *shall be* seven weeks, and threescore and two weeks: the street shall be built again, and the wall, even in troublous times.

Then, it says that the first two segments (49 + 434 = 483 years) would terminate when "Messiah shall be cut off".

Daniel 9:26a = And after [the] threescore and two weeks shall Messiah be cut off, but not for himself...

The Seventy Weeks of Daniel

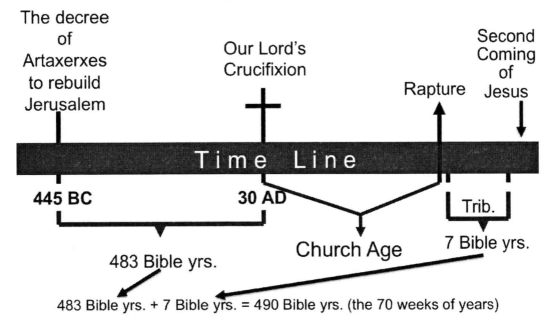

The decree for the Jews taken in the captivity to go back and rebuild Jerusalem was given to Nehemiah by King Artaxerxes of the Persian Empire in 445 BC (Neh. 2:1). Exactly 483 years of 360 days each after this decree was issued, Jesus was crucified just as Daniel's prophecy said.

So, the first two segments of time (the 7 years and the 434 years) have expired. This leaves one final week of years that God said He would deal with the Jewish people. However, in between the 483 years (which ended when Jesus was crucified) and the beginning of the last seven years, would fall the indefinite period of time called the Church Age... AFTER WHICH, the Tribulation (that final seven years) will begin.

In the next verse, Daniel is told WHAT will begin the Tribulation.

Daniel 9:27 - And he [Antichrist] shall confirm the covenant with many for one week: and in the midst of the week he shall cause the sacrifice and the oblation to cease, and for the overspreading of abominations he shall make *it* desolate, even until the consummation, and that determined shall be poured upon the desolate.

So, we see that **the confirming of the covenant** by Antichrist with many of Daniel's people is the event that **will start the Tribulation**. Most Bible scholars believe that this covenant will be some kind of seven-year peace treaty in which Antichrist will promise peace and security for Israel. To simply exist in peace, without the threat of aggression from her neighboring Arab countries, is what Israel has desired since the day she was founded on May 14, 1948.

Now… for whatever reason, people want to push these last days events (the Rapture, the Tribulation, the Millennium, etc.) together "bumper to bumper". In other words, most people don't want to allow for any time lapse between these events. However, there is no Biblical reason for not doing so. There is nothing in the Scriptures to suggest that the Rapture will happen on the same day that Antichrist signs the covenant with Israel… that is, that the end of the Church Age will initiate the start of the Tribulation. For all we know, there could be several days, months, or possibly even years after the Rapture before Antichrist signs the covenant with Israel starting the Tribulation!

Personally, I tend to see it as a period of several MONTHS. A few DAYS would be too short and yet, several YEARS seems to be too long. Why do I say this? Because of what the Bible says will happen in that intervening time period between the Rapture and the Tribulation. For the sake of our discussion on this topic, I will refer to the time period between the Rapture and the Tribulation as the **"Tribulation Prep Period"** because of the things that will occur during that time in preparation for the start of the Tribulation.

Let's look at some of the things that will happen in the "Tribulation Prep Period":

1.   The Rise of Antichrist

Paul tells the church in Thessalonica that they should not be deceived "by any means" into thinking that "the day of Christ" had begun.

2 Thess. 2:1 - Now we beseech you, brethren...

2   That ye be not soon shaken in mind, or be troubled, neither by spirit, nor by word, nor by letter as from us, as that the day of Christ is at hand.

In this context, "the day of Christ" is a reference to the Tribulation. It appears that the church at Thessalonica was under such persecution that they began to think that they had entered into the Tribulation. And, it's possible that they may have even received a forged letter from someone pretending to be Paul saying this since Paul says that they shouldn't be shaken in mind even though they received a "letter as from us".

And then he tells them WHY they could know that the Tribulation had not yet begun. Two things would have to happen first.

2 Thessalonians 2:3 - Let no man deceive you by any means: for *that day shall not come*, except [1] there come a falling away first, and [2] that man of sin be revealed, the son of perdition;

We won't take time here to discuss "the falling away" that Paul mentions, but suffice it to say that preceding the Tribulation, there will come a time of unprecedented apostasy… a time when perhaps millions of people will be led away from the Truth of God's Word into accepting the UNTRUTHS and "doctrines of devils" taught by false prophets and teachers (2 Tim. 4:3). I'm convinced that we are already in that day of apostasy today!

But more to the point of our discussion…
Paul says that before the Tribulation begins, the "man of sin" will be revealed. And he calls him the "Son of Perdition". Without a doubt, this is a reference to the Antichrist.

But what does it mean when it says he shall be "revealed"?

The word is translated from the Greek word "apokalypto" from which we get our English word "apocalypse" and it means "to uncover, lay open what has been veiled or covered up; to make known, make manifest, disclose what before was unknown" [1] In other words, Paul was saying that the Antichrist will become known before the Tribulation. This could mean that he will (1) make his rise to power and be recognized as a great world leader, or (2) be recognized as the true Antichrist described in the Bible.

I prefer to believe he was saying the first... (he will make his rise to power) because any good student of the Bible will recognize him as the Antichrist by the WAY he rises to power (we'll talk about that later).

So, we know that the Antichrist will rise to power before the Tribulation begins. And this makes sense because he must come to power in order to be in a position to negotiate the covenant with Israel. But could it happen before the Rapture also and therefore be BEFORE the "Tribulation Prep Period"? No. Because look what Paul goes on to say in verses 6-8.

2 Thess. 2:6 - And now ye know what withholdeth that he might be revealed in his time.

In other words... Paul says, "You know what it is that is holding back his revealing so that he can be revealed in his time." Or, "at the proper time".

So then, (if they didn't know what was keeping the Antichrist from being revealed) Paul tells them.

2 Thess. 2:7 - For the mystery of iniquity doth already work: only he who now letteth *will let*, until he be taken out of the way.

Paul said that "the mystery of iniquity was ALREADY working."

What is "the mystery of iniquity" (some translations say "mystery of lawlessness")? In 1 Tim. 3:16, the Bible speaks of how magnificent the "mystery of godliness" is and describes it as the life and work of Jesus Christ.

1 Tim. 3:16 - And without controversy great is **the mystery of godliness**: God was manifest in the flesh, justified in the Spirit, seen of angels, preached unto the Gentiles, believed on in the world, received up into glory.

So, if iniquity is the opposite of godliness, then the "mystery of iniquity" must be the opposite of the "mystery of godliness". That is, if the "mystery of godliness" is the life and work of Jesus Christ, then the "mystery of iniquity" must be the life and work of Antichrist... which Paul says was already at work in his day. We might say that the lies and deception that will lead people to accept the Antichrist was already at work in Paul's day. But, the person of Antichrist had not yet appeared because there is Someone who is preventing the debut of Antichrist.

In 2 Thess. 2:7 where Paul says, "only he who now letteth will let, until he be taken out of the way", the word "letteth" in our KJV means "restrains" or "prevents". So, Paul was saying that even though the deception that will be used by the Antichrist was already at work, his debut upon the world scene was being restrained until that restraint is removed. This restraint is a work of the Holy Spirit. It is NOT the Holy Spirit Who is removed during the Tribulation because we know that people will be saved during the Tribulation, and that requires the work of the Holy Spirit. During that time, He will certainly still be on earth doing His work of drawing people to Christ. But *one function* of his present work will be removed... He will no longer restrain (or prevent) the rise of Antichrist. And thus,

2 Thess. 2:8 - And then shall that Wicked be revealed, whom the Lord shall consume with the spirit of his mouth, and shall destroy with the brightness of his coming:

Today, in the Church Age, the Holy Spirit performs many different works (convicting people of their sin and drawing them to Christ, empowering Christians to live in holiness, etc.) And one work that He does is to hold back the tidal wave of wickedness that threatens to cover the planet. How does He do this? He does it by working in and through the lives of the people He possesses (Christians). But when the Church is removed via the Rapture, His restraint will also be removed, allowing sin to flourish and Antichrist to rise to power.

So, since Paul said…
1.   The Antichrist will be revealed BEFORE the Tribulation, and
2.   His rise will be prevented by the Holy Spirit until AFTER the Rapture…

We must conclude that the rise of Antichrist will take place during the Tribulation Prep Period, after the Rapture and before the Tribulation begins.

2. How Antichrist Will Rise to Power

The book of Daniel tells us HOW Antichrist will rise to power.

The prophet Daniel lived during the 70 year captivity of the Jews by King Nebuchadnezzar and the Babylonians. Actually, the Babylonians defeated Jerusalem three times.

1.   605 BC - Babylonians conquer Jerusalem and take some of its wealth and some of its prominent people as slaves to Babylon. Daniel was taken to Babylon in this first deportation.
2.   597 BC - Babylonians conquer Jerusalem the second time and take another 10,000 captives back to Babylon. Ezekiel was taken to Babylon this time.
3.   586 BC - Babylonians utterly destroy Jerusalem and burn the Temple to the ground. King Zedekiah's eyes are gouged out and he is brought to Babylon where he dies. This time, only the poorest and most feeble people are left in Judah to tend the fields.

Daniel was just a teenager when he was taken to Babylon and yet he lived to see the Babylonians defeated by the Medo-Persian Empire. So far as we know, he lived to a ripe old age as a statesman/prophet in Babylon and never returned to Jerusalem.

In the second chapter of Daniel, he relates the story of a disturbing dream that King Nebuchadnezzar had. At this time, Daniel was probably still just a teenager. Yet, he was the only one in the entire empire that could tell Nebuchadnezzar what his dream was and what it meant.

The king's dream was of a statue of a man made of various metals from the head down to the feet of the statue. Daniel interpreted this to Nebuchadnezzar as representing
the four Gentile empires that would rule over Israel throughout history, starting with Nebuchadnezzar's **Babylonian empire**. Later, God also revealed to the prophet the identity of the next three empires. The Babylonians would be followed by the **Medo-Persian** Empire, which would be followed by the **Greek Empire**, which would be followed by the **Roman Empire**. History has proven that this succession was perfectly correct.

In the last part of the interpretation of this dream, Daniel reveals that the last empire represented by the feet of the statue made of a mixture of iron and clay, (the new Roman Empire) would be a resurrection of the old Roman Empire and become the final one… the one that Jesus will destroy at His coming in the end of the age.

Although Daniel's interpretation doesn't say so specifically, we find out in Daniel's later vision in chapter 7 that this new Roman Empire will initially be ruled by ten kings. In Nebuchadnezzar's dream statue, they are represented by the ten toes of the statue. But in Daniel's vision of chapter seven, they are represented as ten horns on the head of the fourth beast that arises out of the sea. The four beasts represent the same four Gentile empires of chapter 2. And Daniel is told that the ten horns on the fourth are "ten kings".

Dan. 7:24a - And the ten horns out of this kingdom *are* ten kings *that* shall arise:

Even though they are referred to as "ten kings", it is more likely that they will be seen as ten "commissioners", or ten politicians in a ruling committee of some sort that will be over ten regions of the new Revived Roman Empire.

As Daniel is looking at this fourth beast with ten horns, suddenly, another little horn grows up in their midst, uprooting three of the ten horns as it comes up.

Dan. 7:8 - I considered the horns, and, behold, there came up among them another little horn, before whom there were three of the first horns plucked up by the roots: and, behold, in this horn *were* eyes like the eyes of man, and a mouth speaking great things.

This "little horn" that arises among the ten commissioners is symbolic of Antichrist. His "eyes of a man" probably speak of him as a visionary or a person of great intellect. And his "mouth speaking great things" tells us that he will be very eloquent and persuasive in his speaking ability. Both of these are good qualities for a successful politician.

In some way (probably some masterful political maneuvering), Antichrist will overthrow three of the ten commissioners. However, in Rev. 17:12-14 we read that the ten kings are still in power when Jesus returns and destroys them.

Rev. 17:12 - And the ten horns which thou sawest are ten kings, which have received no kingdom as yet; but receive power as kings one hour with the beast.

13 These have one mind, and shall give their power and strength unto the beast.

14 These shall make war with the Lamb, and the Lamb shall overcome them: for he is Lord of lords, and King of kings: and they that are with him *are* called, and chosen, and faithful.

So, what is likely to happen is that Antichrist will overthrow the three rulers in his rise to power and then replace them with three more "kings" and make himself the supreme ruler over all ten because they (all 10 of the kings) "shall give their power and strength unto the beast [Antichrist]".

So far, we have discovered that Antichrist will rise to power over the new Revived Roman Empire (a European based empire of nations) AFTER the Rapture, but BEFORE the beginning of the Tribulation (during the Tribulation Prep Period). As he comes up to this top leadership position, he will overthrow three of the ten leaders who control the empire. Now, let's look at WHAT he will do once he has achieved this prestigious position.

3.   The Signing of the Covenant

Even though Antichrist will be a very powerful and persuasive diplomat, convincing both sides to sign the seven-year Middle East Peace Treaty will not be easy. Like all before him who have tried, but failed in establishing a lasting peace treaty between the Jews and Arabs, there will undoubtedly be much talk and negotiations involved in getting this treaty signed. These negotiations will take some time.

In Rev. 13, the Apostle John describes not one, but TWO beasts. In the first ten verses, we have the description of The Beast (the Antichrist). And in verses 11-18, there is a description of a second beast that we know as **The False Prophet**. He is called the False Prophet in three places in the Revelation, Rev. 16:13, 19:20, 20:10.

Rev. 13:11 - And I beheld another beast coming up out of the earth; and he had two horns like a lamb, and he spake as a dragon.

Unlike the first beast (Antichrist) that John sees rising up out of the sea (Rev. 13:1), this beast comes up out of **the earth**. This is obviously symbolic. Also, the four great beasts of Dan.7 come up from **the sea.** Symbolically, the sea represents the gentile nations of the world, which makes sense because the empires of Dan. 7 are *gentile* empires and Antichrist (the first beast) will undoubtedly be a Gentile leader heading a gentile empire. The word "earth" can be a reference to the entire planet, but its first meaning is "arable land". [2] Thus, in contrast to "the sea" (gentile nations), it is likely a reference to the land of Israel. It is for this reason that I believe the False Prophet will be a **Jew** from Israel.

Noteworthy is the picture type of Antichrist in Daniel 11:21-31 in the person of Antiochus Epiphanes, the eighth Selucid Syrian king who was a great persecutor of the Jews. Dr. Ed Hindson notes that "The False Prophet is to the Antichrist what Menelaus was to Antiochus IV. Menelaus was responsible for enforcing many of the Hellenizing decrees of Antiochus IV upon his own people, **the Jews**." [3] (emphasis mine) Menelaus was a Jewish High Priest during the time that Antiochus was king of Syria. So, as a Jew who worked with Antiochus, he is a picture of the False Prophet who will likely also be a Jew who works with the Antichrist.

Notice the anti-types that Satan and his cohorts present:

1.   As there is a Holy Trinity… Father, Son, and Holy Spirit, there is an Unholy Trinity… Satan, Antichrist, and False Prophet.

2.   Satan is the Anti-God.
         The Beast is the Anti-Christ.
         The False Prophet is the Anti-Spirit.

3.   Just as Jesus is the Son of God, Antichrist will be the Son of Satan.

4.   Just as the Holy Spirit was sent from the Holy Father (John 14:16), Satan will send the False Prophet. This explains why even though he has two horns (symbolic of his power) like a lamb, i.e., very humble and unassuming, he will "speak as a dragon" … that dragon being Satan (Rev. 12:9).

Also, Rev. 13:13 tells us that the False Prophet will have supernatural powers, even the ability to call down fire from heaven.

Rev. 13:13 - And he doeth great wonders, so that he maketh fire come down from heaven on the earth in the sight of men,

But this should not be a surprise since Satan has that same power (Job 1:16).

5.   Just as the work of the Holy Spirit is to point people to the second person of the Holy Trinity, Jesus Christ, the work of the False Prophet will be to point people to the second person of the Unholy Trinity, the Antichrist.

Rev. 13:12 - And he exerciseth all the power of the first beast before him, and **causeth the earth and them which dwell therein to worship the first beast**, whose deadly wound was healed.

6.   The Bible says that all three persons of the Unholy Trinity (Satan, Antichrist, and the False Prophet) will be thrown ALIVE into the eternal Lake of Fire. (Rev. 19:20, 20:10)

7.   Just as the Holy Spirit seals the followers of Christ until the day of redemption (Eph. 4:30), the False Prophet will seal the followers of Antichrist until the day of condemnation (Rev. 13:16-17).

Rev. 13:16 - And he causeth all, both small and great, rich and poor, free and bond, to receive a mark in their right hand, or in their foreheads:

So, from these points and many others that could be made showing the connection between Antichrist and the False Prophet, it is clear that they will work closely together on the agenda of Antichrist. And since we believe that the False Prophet will be a Jew from Israel, it is likely that he will have great influence and will lead Israel to accept the Antichrist covenant. In fact, he may even be involved in the negotiations of the treaty.

<u>Summary</u>

In summary, what we've learned from this lesson is this:

(NOTE - The DETAILS here may be somewhat speculative, but the overall events are biblically supported.)

1.   When the last person has been saved and the Church is complete, Jesus will come for His Church in that glorious event that we call the Rapture.

2.   In the previous lesson, we learned that the Rapture will create a day of terrible destruction, upheaval, and chaos. For a short period of time, anarchy will reign as nations try to recover from the sudden disappearance of millions of their citizens. This day of chaos and confusion will present the perfect environment for Mr. Antichrist to rise to the top of the European Revived Roman Empire.

3.   His sudden popularity will cause him to be haled as the "answer" for Europe's problem. People will love him so much that it will go beyond just "loyalty to their new leader" and will border on actual *worship* of this extremely charismatic politician.

4.   Yet, perhaps because of jealousy, at least three of the ten European commissioners will oppose him.

5.   But through some deceptive political maneuvering, he will manage to destroy the political careers of those three leaders and they will be removed from office. It is possible that they will be assassinated, but it is more likely that they will just lose their office through some scandalous revelation about their personal or political lives. This will allow Antichrist to threaten the other seven commissioners with similar consequences if they don't support him. He will then hand-pick three successors to the three who are overthrown and they will be quickly elected by his adoring followers in the European political establishment. At the same time, he will be appointed as the President of the whole Commission.

6.   Quite possibly, because of the small percentage of the Europeans who are true Christians, the disruption by the Rapture will not be as severe as it is in other nations of the world. Nevertheless, the already impending collapse of their economic system will be greatly exacerbated by the Rapture. So, with his eloquent speech, he will reassure his citizens that he is able to restore order and prosperity. He will have a plan to get the empire back on track and the people will accept his plan.

7.   As has been the case throughout his life and political career, his actions as the Supreme Leader of the European empire will be very successful. And as the citizens begin to enjoy their new prosperity, they will love Antichrist even more. And other nations of the world will begin to see him as THE example of great leadership.

8.   Nations outside of the European empire will continue the struggle to regain order, civil freedoms, and economic prosperity. Bordering nations to the empire will desire to join the Antichrist's confederacy of nations… his empire… and thus, his borders will spread quickly to the Middle East and probably northern Africa since this is the same territory that was controlled by the Roman Empire.

9.   As Antichrist addresses the United Nations General Assembly and the eyes of the world are upon him, he will point to his successes in the European economy and claim that if given the opportunity, he can do the same thing for ALL the nations of the world. Because of the lingering frustrations among the world's national leaders, they will see a bright ray of hope in Premier Antichrist. His promises of world peace and prosperity will catapult him to great fame and prominence among the leaders of the world.

10.   Then, to put the crowning touches on his political achievements and really draw many other nations into his coalition empire, he does something that many have failed at doing… something that most of the world had come to believe was impossible. Using his power, influence, and great diplomatic skills, he convinces the Jews in Israel and their neighboring Arab nations to sign a seven-year peace treaty.

In that treaty, Israel will be recognized as a Jewish state and will be given the promise of a peaceful existence. The Arab nations will probably be promised great prosperity through international trade and will be threatened with military defeat if they refuse it. And then, to "seal the deal", both sides agree to a "sharing arrangement" of the Temple Mount in Jerusalem that will allow the Arabs to keep their Dome of the Rock and the Jews to build their Third Temple.

11.   It is very possible that the Israeli side of this treaty will be negotiated by a great Rabbi in Israel who will eventually become the "right hand man" of Antichrist known in the Bible as the False Prophet.

12.   The seven-year Middle East Peace Treaty will be heralded as the greatest diplomatic accomplishment in history. International media announcements about the day of its signing will have the whole world looking in as the dignitaries gather in Jerusalem. Perhaps with great fanfare and celebration, each leader will step to the documents table and sign his name. At the signing of the last name (probably that of Antichrist as a crescendo to the whole event), the world neither hears it nor notices anything unusual, but amid all the applause, hand shaking, and picture taking, in God's great spiritual realm… BOOM! The divine clock is started. The seven years of The Tribulation has begun!

If you have not been truly born again into the family of God…
If you have not given your life to Christ, repented of your sins, and asked Him for eternal life, it is very possible that the Rapture could happen and you would be left behind.

And since you have read and have been taught in this lesson what will happen in the Tribulation Prep Period after the Rapture, you will remember this information with great sadness, fear, and trepidation. As each event unfolds just as the Bible has said that it will, you will know that you are about to enter into the worst time of all human history. A time when Jesus said,

Matt. 24:21 - For then shall be great tribulation, such as was not since the beginning of the world to this time, no, nor ever shall be.

22.   And except those days should be shortened, there should no flesh be saved…

If you have not made your heart right with Jesus Christ and asked for the salvation that He offers as a free gift, you are running a terrible risk! Before I can finish this next sentence, the trumpet could sound… all the true Christians would be snatched away in an instant… and you would be left to contemplate the horrors of the Tribulation that will soon come.

So, don't be a fool! Secure your salvation today!

(1) http://www.blbclassic.org/lang/lexicon/lexicon.cfm?Strongs=G601&t=KJV
(2) http://www.blueletterbible.org/lang/lexicon/lexicon.cfm?Strongs=G1093&t=KJV
(3)   Tim LaHaye and Ed Hindson, *The Popular Encyclopedia of Bible Prophecy,* (OR: Harvest House Publishers, 2004) p. 103

Between the Rapture and the Tribulation

Lesson 2 Quiz

1.   The Rapture is not the initiating event of the Tribulation. It is the concluding event of the _____ _____.

2.   In Daniel 9:24, God tells the prophet that He is going to deal with Daniel's people for another _____ weeks, which is _____ years.

3.   And, what event does God say will start this time period?

4.   All but the last week of years has been completed. So, the last week of years is sometimes referred to as _____ _____ week.

5.   The event that starts the seven year Tribulation is what?

6.   According to 2 Thess. 2, the rise of Antichrist to become the head of the new Revived Roman Empire will happen [before, after] the Rapture of the Church.

7.   The Babylonians conquered Jerusalem and destroyed the Temple in what year?

8.   The Revived Roman Empire that Antichrist will eventually head up, will initially be lead by how many "kings"?

9.   According to Daniel 7, Antichrist will come to power by overthrowing how many of those original kings?

10.   The second beast described in Rev. 13 as having "two horns like a lamb, and he spake like a dragon" is the one we call what?

Between the Rapture and the Tribulation

Lesson 2 Quiz Answers

1.   Church Age

2.   70, 490

3.   The decree to rebuild the city of Jerusalem.

4.   Daniel's Seventieth

5.   The confirming of the covenant by the Antichrist with Israel.

6.   after

7.   586 BC

8.   ten

9.   three

10. The False Prophet

What Happens After the Rapture?

Lesson 3
The First Half of the Tribulation

As we discussed in the previous lessons, the Rapture of the Church will come suddenly and unexpectedly, plunging the world into chaos and confusion. But, from this time of unparalleled anarchy and planetary disruption, an extremely charismatic politician will rise to power in Europe. He will be the Antichrist.

Through his excellent abilities of speech and persuasion, he will garner the support and admiration of most of the planet. And, from his position as the Supreme Leader of the most powerful geopolitical entity on Earth (the Revived Roman Empire), he will negotiate a seven-year peace plan in the Middle East between Israel and the Muslim nations. On the day… At the very moment the signatures are made on the documents of this peace treaty, God's clock will start on Daniel's Seventieth Week… the day of the Tribulation.

Now, in this lesson, we will discuss the events of the first half of the Tribulation… the first three and one half years of the seven years. And since the book of Revelation is our greatest God-given information source for the things that will happen in the Tribulation, we will use it as our Guide Book.

First, let's discuss some of the keys to understanding the book of Revelation. Notice the following:

1.   God did not give us the Revelation to simply make the Bible a thicker book! As the last book of the Bible, it is the final revelation of how the story of mankind will end. And the good news is that JESUS WINS! And God WANTS us to know that!

And not only that, but He wants us to know many of the details of the events that will make up the last chapters of mortal human history. Of course, He doesn't tell us EVERYTHING. But He tells us a lot.

What's more, because He created us… and because He knows better than anyone how our minds operate… and because He loves us more that we can even understand and wants the very best for us… He would NOT give us the information in Revelation if He thought it would be BAD for us. Nor would He give us the Revelation if He knew it would be impossible for us to understand it! He WANTS us to read and understand the book of Revelation and be blessed by it. He even promises a blessing to those who read and do the things written in it.

Rev. 1:3 - Blessed *is* he that readeth, and they that hear the words of this prophecy, and keep those things which are written therein: for the time *is* at hand.

2.   **The Revelation IS understandable** for every born again believer who has a desire in his heart to understand it.

Some Christians claim that all of the symbolism in Revelation makes it impossible to understand. That is NOT so!

It is true that Revelation contains more symbolic language than any other book of the Bible. But God did this for a reason… and that reason was NOT to confuse us or give us some mysterious piece of literature that is so beyond our understanding that it is of no use to us.

In the very first verse of the book, God tells us that it is a book of SIGNS.

Rev. 1:1 - The Revelation of Jesus Christ, which God gave unto him, to shew unto his servants things which must shortly come to pass; and he sent and **signified *it*** by his angel unto his servant John:

Think of that word "signified" as "sign-i-fied". God, in His great omniscience, decided it would be best to relate this "final days information" to us in signs (or, symbolic language) for a reason. Why? Because in that way, only God's people would really understand what it was saying! To the lost world, it is a mysterious, impossible-to-understand book. And even when they do try to understand it, they get it all wrong and mixed up! That's why we have so many "Apocalypse" movies that supposedly are based on the Bible, and yet they are nothing more than figments of man's imagination.

You see, the Revelation is extremely important and relevant to us last days Christians. But it is ONLY for us to understand... NOT for the carnal minded! Moses revealed this principle to the children of Israel when he delivered God's commandments to them. He said,

Deut. 29:29 - The secret *things belong* unto the LORD our God: but those *things which are* revealed *belong* unto us and to our children for ever, that *we* may do all the words of this law.

When God finished the prophetic revelations that He gave to Daniel, He told the prophet to close up and seal his book because those prophecies were not for Daniel's time.

Dan. 12:9 - And he said, Go thy way, Daniel: for the words *are* closed up and sealed **till the time of the end**.

That is, only the people living at "the time of the end" will be able to understand Daniel's prophecies. And even then, it wouldn't be for ALL people to understand because he says in the very next verse,

Dan. 12:10b - ...**and none of the wicked shall understand; but the wise shall understand.**

And that understanding will come at "the time of the end". Therefore, when we get to Revelation, God says near the end of the book...

Rev. 22:10 - And he saith unto me, Seal not the sayings of the prophecy of this book: for the time is at hand.

So, when you and I read the prophecies of the end time in the books of Daniel and Revelation (and other prophecies of God's Word), we are reading about things God WANTS us to understand. And He wrote the Revelation so that the wise would understand it, but the wicked world of our day would not.

It has been said that Daniel is the Revelation of the Old Testament. Without a doubt, without a good understanding of Daniel, it is very hard to understand Revelation. The prophecies of God that are "enfolded" in Daniel and "unfolded" in Revelation.

So, God uses symbols to hide the truth of Revelation from the unsaved. But to the Christian who knows God's Word, behind every symbol is a plain sense meaning... a meaning that the world at large does not see. But it is something that God does want His people to know.

3.   Basically, the Revelation is written in chronological order... with a few exceptions. There are certain "intervals", or parenthetical passages, that are scattered through the book of Revelation that jump back in time (a "flash-back"), or ahead in time (a "flash-forward").

The **flash-backs** usually give us past information that provides the background information that we need to understand the information we're reading at that time.

The **flash-forwards** are usually for encouragement. Because Revelation is so filled with pain, destruction, and bloodshed, it is as though God wants to jump ahead and show us the victory in the end so we don't get discouraged and give up.

And sometimes, the interval passage is just a larger overview designed to help us see the "bigger picture".

In any case, these "Interval Passages" are sometimes difficult to recognize, but a persistent study will help the reader to eventually see them and understand their purpose.

Rev. 1:19 gives us the basic content format of the book of Revelation.

Rev. 1:19 - Write the things which thou hast seen, and the things which are, and the things which shall be hereafter;

So, we see here that there are three basic divisions of Revelation:

1.   "the things which thou hast seen" - The past (Rev. 1)
2.   "the things which are" - The present (Rev. 2-3)
3.   "the things which shall be hereafter" - The future (Rev. 4-22)

From the time that John was writing the Revelation on the Isle of Patmos, "the things that he had seen" refers to his vision of The Son of Man coming to him… that is, his appearance, what He said, etc.

"The things which are" refers to the seven letters that John was told to write to the seven churches in Asia Minor. These churches were actual Christian churches that existed in John's day. However, a close look at the seven letters will reveal that each of the letters actually describe seven sequential time periods in the Church Age that define what THE Church would be like, ending with the Laodicean Church having the characteristics of spiritual "lukewarmness".

Then, beginning in chapter 4, we have the beginning of "the things which shall be hereafter". It is a description of how John is called up to heaven… a picture type of the Rapture.

Rev. 4:1 - After this I looked, and, behold, a door *was* opened in heaven: and the first voice which I heard *was* as it were of a trumpet talking with me; which said, Come up hither, and I will shew thee **things which must be hereafter**.

At this point, John is carried away into Heaven and into the very throne room of God Almighty. Around God's throne are four mighty angelic creatures and 24 elders seated on their thrones.

In the hand of God is a scroll sealed with seven seals.

Rev. 5:2 - And I saw a strong angel proclaiming with a loud voice, Who is worthy to open the book, and to loose the seals thereof?

At first, it seems that no one is able to receive the scroll and break its seals to open it. But then,

Rev. 5:6a - And I beheld, and, lo, in the midst of the throne and of the four beasts, and in the midst of the elders, stood a Lamb as it had been slain...

This Lamb is none other than Jesus Christ, the Son of God, the Lamb Who was slain for the sins of the world. The Lord went to God's throne and took the scroll from the hand of God. Contained within the book is the revelation of God's program and purpose for the Tribulation.

Seal Judgments No. 1-4 - The Four Horsemen of the Apocalypse

So, beginning in chapter 6, with the breaking of the first seal, we begin to read about the cataclysmic events that are brought upon the earth as each individual seal is broken. During the Tribulation, the **seven seals** are followed by **seven trumpet** blowings, which are followed by the pouring out of **seven bowls** of God's wrath. Altogether, these represent 21 judgments of God (great disastrous events) that He will bring upon the inhabitants of earth during the Tribulation. In this lesson, we will look at the first 14 of these judgments (the "seal" and "trumpet" judgments) along with some other events that are described that will happen in the first half (first 3 ½ years) of the Tribulation.

The breaking of the first four seals brings four successive horseback riders into John's view. With each one, there is symbolism representing horrible hardship that befalls the people on earth. We will look at each one of them individually, but first something must be said of all four as a group.

Time wise, the representations of "The Four Horsemen of the Apocalypse" (as they are sometimes called) covers the entire seven-year Tribulation. As we will see, the actions of each one come as a result of the actions of the one preceding it. So, they are integrally tied together as a "group succession" and that total process covers the entire seven years.

Essentially, the four represent war, bloodshed, famine & disease, and ultimately death. These will be characteristics that start at the beginning of the Tribulation with war and culminate at its end with a massive, worldwide, death toll. So, it would not be possible to delineate which of the four occur in the first half of the Tribulation and which ones follow in the last half. Nor would it be correct to assume that all four occur in the first half and cease at the midpoint just because they are given to us as a group succession that begins the 21 judgments. Therefore, let us look at them as a succession of afflictions from God, each one leading into the next, that characterizes the events of the whole Tribulation.

Shortly after the signing of the seven-year peace treaty with Israel, the ambitions of the Antichrist will push him to expand the borders of his empire. So strong will be those ambitions that he will begin to use military aggression to take control of neighboring nations. But this is not how he starts out before the Tribulation.

In describing the "willful king" (Antichrist) in Daniel 11:21, the Scriptures tell us "he shall come in peaceably, and obtain the kingdom by flatteries". And for those who work with him and are loyal to him, "he shall cause them to rule over many, and shall divide the land for gain." (Dan. 11:39). In other words, prior to the Tribulation, during the Tribulation Prep Period as Antichrist rises to power and strengthens his empire, he will use peaceable means (non-military means) to establish himself. But no doubt, lying, cheating, bribery, and "under the table" pay-offs will be a large part of his "modus operandi".

But after the signing of the treaty, his methods become even more sinister as he just begins to TAKE what he wants… including whole countries. How do we know this? Because the breaking of the first seal describes him.

Rev. 6:2 - And I saw, and behold a white horse: and he that sat on him had a bow; and a crown was given unto him: and he went forth conquering, and to conquer.

The rider of this white horse is NOT Jesus Who also comes to earth in Rev. 19 riding a white stallion as the KING OF KINGS AND LORD OF LORDS (Rev. 19:11-16). This rider wears a crown (a "stephanos" in the Greek, meaning a wreath signifying victory) that is different from the crown that Jesus wears (a "diadem" crown of royalty).

The white horse rider is symbolic of the Antichrist who starts the Tribulation by going "forth conquering, and to conquer". The fact that he rides a WHITE horse and wears a "stephanos" crown says that he is victorious in his conquests. The fact that he carries a bow, but no arrows are mentioned may mean that some of his achievements come as a result of his show of power, but do not require bloodshed... at least at first. Because then the second seal is broken...

Rev. 6:4 - And there went out another horse *that was* red: and *power* was given to him that sat thereon to take peace from the earth, and that they should kill one another: and there was given unto him a great sword.

At some point in his conquests, the Antichrist's aggression turns bloody. Red is symbolic of blood and whether this rider is a literal person who starts a bloody war, or is symbolic the "spirit of warfare" is immaterial. The result is the same. Peace is taken away and in its place comes one with "a great sword", the symbol of war. Notice how widespread this warfare is. It says that peace is taken "from the earth". All around the globe, war will rage.

In His Olivet Discourse, Jesus said that the last days would be characterized by "wars and rumors of wars" (Matt. 24:6). But by the time the red horse rider comes on the scene during the Tribulation, the rumors will have come true. It will seem that all over the planet, nations are engaging in warfare.

Rev. 6:5 - And when he had opened the third seal, I heard the third beast say, Come and see. And I beheld, and lo a black horse; and he that sat on him had a pair of balances in his hand.

6   And I heard a voice in the midst of the four beasts say, A measure of wheat for a penny, and three measures of barley for a penny; and *see* thou hurt not the oil and the wine.

As warfare always does, the land, the manufacturing of agricultural equipment, and the harvest of crops is redirected to the war efforts. Consequently, food production suffers great reduction and starvation ensues. Black is the symbolic color of famine. Verse 6 describes a situation where an entire day's wage will be required to buy a very small quantity of wheat or barley, hardly enough to feed one person for a day. And the last phrase indicates a time of exorbitant prices for every day items like oil and wine.

Rev. 6:8 - And I looked, and behold a pale horse: and his name that sat on him was Death, and Hell followed with him. And power was given unto them over the fourth part of the earth, to kill with sword, and with hunger, and with death, and with the beasts of the earth.

Finally, we read of the PALE horse rider. The idea of a "pale" horse is a bit unusual for us. This word in the original Greek is the word "chloros", which means a yellowish-green color. It is the color of a dead body that has lost the pinkish hue of blood flowing through it. It is the color of death.

After all the war, bloodshed, and famine, then starvation and disease will become endemic. The horrible scenes of history where death has closed its grip on multitudes of people, leaving heaps of bodies to decay in the hot sun will pale in comparison to the widespread death of the final days of the Tribulation. No part of the planet will be spared from these horrors. Pain, heartache, and death will be common to every nation, region, and municipality. And in some places, there will be so much death that the sanitation services that remove the bodies will not be able to keep up. The scripture says that one fourth of the planet will die.

Then, to add to the gruesomeness of the whole scene, wild beasts (scavengers of every sort) will gorge themselves on the rotting flesh.

These "Four Horsemen of the Apocalypse" represented in the unleashing of the first four seal judgments are one of the "interval passages" that I spoke of earlier… one that is given as an overview of a larger span of time. It would be difficult to place the horrors brought on by these four horsemen as happening only in the first half of the Tribulation. Instead, these four seals cover the entire period of the seven years of Tribulation.

The first horseman (the Antichrist going out to make war) will initiate the seven years. But at what time the following three start during the Tribulation is an unknown. The idea of these first four seals is to give an overview of all the war, famine, and death that will prevail during the seven years. Therefore, even though we could say that the first four seal judgments happen in sequential order, the following judgments will be happening during that same time frame.

Seal Judgment No. 5 - The Martyrs' Complaint

Rev. 6:9 - And when he had opened the fifth seal, I saw under the altar the souls of them that were slain for the word of God, and for the testimony which they held:

10   And they cried with a loud voice, saying, How long, O Lord, holy and true, dost thou not judge and avenge our blood on them that dwell on the earth?

11   And white robes were given unto every one of them; and it was said unto them, that they should rest yet for a little season, until their fellowservants also and their brethren, that should be killed as they *were*, should be fulfilled.

Next, our attention is drawn back to a heavenly event. When the fifth seal is broken, John sees the "souls of them that were slain for the word of God, and for the testimony which they held".

There are a few points to be made about this group:

1. That they are seen underneath the altar is a reference to the sacrificial altar in the heavenly tabernacle. This signifies that they were given as a sacrifice unto the Lord… that is, martyrs of their faith.

2. The fact that they are seen as "souls" supports our understanding of the biblical definition of physical death. That is, when a person dies the physical death, that part of him that is eternal (the soul and spirit) departs from the body. The body then goes back to the dust from which it came. But, as a Christian, in his soul/spirit form, he goes to heaven where he awaits for the day of the Resurrection when he will get a new, glorified body (1 Thess. 4:16, 1 Cor. 15:35-50). This will happen at the time of the Rapture.

   Since they have not yet received their new, glorified body and yet they are seen in the Tribulation AFTER the Rapture, it is obvious that they died DURING the Tribulation.

3. As martyrs of their faith, they have suffered the ultimate sacrifice for their Lord for which they will receive a special crown (Rev. 2:8-11). In heaven, this recognition will be highly valued.

Persecution of Christians unto death will soon follow the Rapture. In the last half of the Tribulation, we know that those who will not bow down and worship the image of the Antichrist will be persecuted unto death (Rev. 13:15), but here we see that martyrdom will also occur early on in the Tribulation. This tells me that persecution of Christians will have already become quite severe by the time of the Rapture and will lead to martyrdom shortly afterward. But since Antichrist rises to power shortly after the Rapture, it is not likely that he will be doing the persecuting. Who then?

As in the Dark Ages, the persecution will come from the ecclesiastical church (Rev. 17:6).

When they ask the Lord how long their blood will not be avenged on earth, they are told to wait "a little season" (perhaps the remainder of the Tribulation) until the rest of the martyrs were killed.

Seal Judgment No. 6 - The Physical Upheaval

Rev. 6:12 - And I beheld when he had opened the sixth seal, and, lo, there was a great earthquake; and the sun became black as sackcloth of hair, and the moon became as blood;

13   And the stars of heaven fell unto the earth, even as a fig tree casteth her untimely figs, when she is shaken of a mighty wind.

14   And the heaven departed as a scroll when it is rolled together; and every mountain and island were moved out of their places.

15   And the kings of the earth, and the great men, and the rich men, and the chief captains, and the mighty men, and every bondman, and every free man, hid themselves in the dens and in the rocks of the mountains;

16   And said to the mountains and rocks, Fall on us, and hide us from the face of him that sitteth on the throne, and from the wrath of the Lamb:

17   For the great day of his wrath is come; and who shall be able to stand?

At some point during the first half of the Tribulation, God will unleash an enormous earthquake on earth. Perhaps, it will cause volcanoes to erupt, spewing millions of tons of dust into the atmosphere, which in turn will cause the light of the sun to be blocked out and the moon, on the other side of the earth will appear blood red from the sun shining through the dust and debris in the atmosphere.

At the same time, immense meteorite showers will blast through the atmosphere ("the stars of heaven fell unto the earth"). Everybody, regardless of their position in society, will be terrified and will recognize these cataclysmic events as judgment from God. But instead of repenting of their sins and crying out to God for forgiveness, they pray for the mountains and rocks to hide them from the Lord's wrath.

Interval of Rev. 7

Chapter 7 begins with the words, "And after these things..." which refers to the massive physical upheaval described in the last part of chapter 6. After that great upheaval, the earth is covered with an eerie silence as the wind completely stops.

Rev. 7:1 - And after these things I saw four angels standing on the four corners of the earth, holding the four winds of the earth, that the wind should not blow on the earth, nor on the sea, nor on any tree.

Rev. 7:2-8 describes God picking out 144,000 special servants, 12,000 from each of the twelve tribes of Israel. Because they are God's servants, they will undoubtedly be witnesses of His great power and love as they go about proclaiming the Gospel of the Kingdom throughout the earth. And as a result, multitudes of people will come to know Christ as their Savior. Perhaps, we might even speculate that the martyrs mentioned in Chapter 6 are part of this great harvest of souls.

I have often been asked if people will be saved during the Tribulation. The answer is yes. There will be a great harvest of souls in the midst of that unprecedented suffering, but most of those will be persecuted unto death.

Why does God do this? Because it is in fulfillment of something Jesus said in Matthew 24.

Matt. 24:14 - And this gospel of the kingdom shall be preached in all the world for a witness unto all nations; and then shall the end come.

Before Jesus returns at the end of the Tribulation to destroy the enemies of God, God will see to it that every single person on earth has heard the Gospel of the Kingdom and had a chance to repent of their sins and receive Christ. Part of that work will be fulfilled by the preaching of the 144,000 Jewish servants.

Contrary to the teaching of some, these 144,000 servants are NOT the number of the believers who end up in Heaven. Through the Scriptures' specific identification of 12,000 from each of the twelve tribes of Israel, God leaves no doubt about who these men are. They are 144,000 specially chosen servants of God who are JEWS. Their job will be to preach the Gospel of the Kingdom "in all the world for a witness unto all nations; and then shall the end come.".

What will be the results of this preaching? A great multitude which no man could number will go to Heaven!

Rev. 7:9 - After this I beheld, and, lo, a great multitude, which no man could number, of all nations, and kindreds, and people, and tongues, stood before the throne, and before the Lamb, clothed with white robes, and palms in their hands;

10   And cried with a loud voice, saying, Salvation to our God which sitteth upon the throne, and unto the Lamb.

[skipping to verse 13]

13   And one of the elders answered, saying unto me, What are these which are arrayed in white robes? and whence came they?

14   And I said unto him, Sir, thou knowest. And he said to me, These are they which came out of great tribulation, and have washed their robes, and made them white in the blood of the Lamb.

Preachers are quick to talk about the HORRORS of the Tribulation. But we often fail to talk about the HARVEST of the Tribulation. During the Tribulation, a numberless multitude will come to know the Lord Jesus as their Savior. But, here once again, we see that they are in heaven DURING the Tribulation, which means they died during the Tribulation. Their deaths will come as a result of the persecution, the enormous plagues sent by God, crime, and warfare.

Seal Judgment No. 7 – The Seven Trumpet Judgments

Rev. 8:1 - And when he had opened the seventh seal, there was silence in heaven about the space of half an hour.

2   And I saw the seven angels which stood before God; and to them were given seven trumpets...

[skipping down to verse 5]

5   And the angel took the censer, and filled it with fire of the altar, and cast *it* into the earth: and there were voices, and thunderings, and lightnings, and an earthquake.

6   And the seven angels which had the seven trumpets prepared themselves to sound.

The opening of the seventh seal once again causes an earthquake with lightning and thunder. It is as if God is getting everyone's attention for an announcement… And that announcement is that the seven trumpet judgments are about to begin.

Trumpet Judgment No. 1 - Fire and Brimstone

Rev. 8:7 - The first angel sounded, and there followed hail and fire mingled with blood, and they were cast upon the earth: and the third part of trees was burnt up, and all green grass was burnt up.

One third of the planet's vegetation is consumed in fire that rains down from heaven.

Trumpet Judgment No. 2 - The Great Meteorite

Rev. 8:8 - And the second angel sounded, and as it were a great mountain burning with fire was cast into the sea: and the third part of the sea became blood;

9   And the third part of the creatures which were in the sea, and had life, died; and the third part of the ships were destroyed.

A mountain size meteorite crashed into the sea, killing one third of the sea creatures and destroying one third of the ships that were in the sea. Such a catastrophe cannot be imagined.

Trumpet Judgment No. 3 - Wormwood

Rev. 8:10 - And the third angel sounded, and there fell a great star from heaven, burning as it were a lamp, and it fell upon the third part of the rivers, and upon the fountains of waters;

11   And the name of the star is called Wormwood: and the third part of the waters became wormwood; and many men died of the waters, because they were made bitter.

Another great meteorite named Wormwood comes crashing down on earth. Where it hits, we do not know. But the results were that it caused a third of the world's fresh water to become poisoned and many men died from drinking that poisoned water.

Trumpet Judgment No. 4 - Darkness

Rev. 8:12 - And the fourth angel sounded, and the third part of the sun was smitten, and the third part of the moon, and the third part of the stars; so as the third part of them was darkened, and the day shone not for a third part of it, and the night likewise.

The earth is plunged into 8 hours of absolute darkness. For one third of the day (one third of 12 = 4) and one third of the night (one third of 12 = 4), the celestial bodies do not shine. Nothing accentuates pain like total darkness!

Before the next three judgments fall, the inhabitants of earth are warned that they will be even worse that what has already been experienced. An angel declares them to be "Three Woes"!

Rev. 8;13 - And I beheld, and heard an angel flying through the midst of heaven, saying with a loud voice, Woe, woe, woe, to the inhabiters of the earth by reason of the other voices of the trumpet of the three angels, which are yet to sound!

Trumpet Judgment No. 5 - Stinging Locusts (The First Woe)

Rev. 9:1 - And the fifth angel sounded, and I saw a star fall from heaven unto the earth: and to him was given the key of the bottomless pit.

2   And he opened the bottomless pit; and there arose a smoke out of the pit, as the smoke of a great furnace; and the sun and the air were darkened by reason of the smoke of the pit.

3   And there came out of the smoke locusts upon the earth: and unto them was given power, as the scorpions of the earth have power.

4   And it was commanded them that they should not hurt the grass of the earth, neither any green thing, neither any tree; but only those men which have not the seal of God in their foreheads.

5   And to them it was given that they should not kill them, but that they should be tormented five months: and their torment *was* as the torment of a scorpion, when he striketh a man.

6   And in those days shall men seek death, and shall not find it; and shall desire to die, and death shall flee from them.

[skipping down to verse 12]

12   One woe is past; *and*, behold, there come two woes more hereafter.

When the fifth trumpet is sounded, an angel opens the bottomless pit and a great blast of smoke comes belching out... so large and thick that it blocked out the light of the sun.

Suddenly, a great roaring is heard like the sound of a thousand helicopters, as millions of "locust demons" come flying out of the smoke. We know that they are a demonic army because they have king over them named Apollyon who commands them to not hurt the vegetation, but only the people who do not have the seal of God in their foreheads (the 144,000 special servants, Rev. 7:3).

They flood into every direction of the sky, bent on doing their horrible duty to inflict as much pain as they can. In their scorpion-like tails they have a sting that is unbelievably painful, like that of ten rattlesnakes, such that people want to die when they are stung, the pain is so horrendous.

Soon, as the first victims are attacked, emergency channels are flooded with the news of this horrible scourge. People sit in fear, locked in their homes, as they hear the approaching monsters. But no one can stay inside indefinitely as the swarms constantly circle about for the next five months. But for those who venture out for food or water, pain worse than death awaits them.

But then, after five months of torturing people, just as quickly as they came, they're gone. Not one is in sight. "One woe is past, but two more are coming!"

Trumpet Judgment No. 6 - The 200,000,000 Man Army (The Second Woe)

Rev. 9:13 - And the sixth angel sounded, and I heard a voice from the four horns of the golden altar which is before God,

14   Saying to the sixth angel which had the trumpet, Loose the four angels which are bound in the great river Euphrates.

15   And the four angels were loosed, which were prepared for an hour, and a day, and a month, and a year, for to slay the third part of men.

16   And the number of the army of the horsemen *were* two hundred thousand thousand: and I heard the number of them.

[skipping down to verse 20]

20   And the rest of the men which were not killed by these plagues yet repented not of the works of their hands, that they should not worship devils, and idols of gold, and silver, and brass, and stone, and of wood: which neither can see, nor hear, nor walk:

For those who have been an eye witness to the horrors of war, they understand the awful evil of warfare. They understand how men can become so wicked that human life means absolutely nothing to them. But of THIS army, even hardened veterans of war cannot imagine such overwhelming bloodshed... ONE THIRD OF HUMANITY! If there are 8 billion people on earth today, that would amount two and two thirds billion people!

The appearance of this demonic horde defies description. But John, using the best of his language skills said that they ride horses that had heads like lions that belched forth fire, smoke, and brimstone. Their serpent-like tails had heads that inflict great destruction. Riding upon these horses were warriors wearing fiery breastplates. The fear from just looking upon such horrid creatures is overwhelming as they go through cities, towns, villages, and countryside killing every human in sight. This is the Second Woe.

And yet, even with that, the people who were not killed, STILL refused to repent of their sins!

Chapter 10 is another interval passage, so we will skip it for now and start with it in the next lesson.

Chapter 11 describes for us some other servants of God that will work in the first half of the Tribulation. They are

The Two Great Witnesses

Rev. 11:3 - And I will give *power* unto my two witnesses, and they shall prophesy a thousand two hundred *and* threescore days, [1260 days] clothed in sackcloth.

[skipping to vs. 5]

5   And if any man will hurt them, fire proceedeth out of their mouth, and devoureth their enemies: and if any man will hurt them, he must in this manner be killed.

During the first half of the Tribulation, the two great witnesses of God will operate out of Jerusalem. Rev. 11:4 says they prophesy for 1260 days, which is 3 ½ year, undoubtedly, the first half of the Tribulation.

Their bold message of repentance will arouse great anger among the people. But no one is able to kill them because God gives them supernatural power to speak fire upon those who try. They also have the supernatural power to cause great droughts and to turn fresh water sources into blood, not fit for consumption or even irrigation. In addition to this, they have the power to call down all sorts of plagues on mankind. So, the inhabitants of the world hate them.

When they are finished preaching the messages that God has given them, the Antichrist will manage to kill them. But he does not bury them. Their dead bodies are allowed to lie in the streets of Jerusalem for three and a half days, during which time, people all over the world will rejoice and celebrate their death.

But then, with the eyes of the world fixed upon them, they are resurrected back to life and a mighty voice from Heaven says, "Come up hither!" And as the world stares at them in fear and disbelief, they ascend into the clouds, out of sight.

Suddenly, another great earthquake shakes Jerusalem, killing 7,000 people. Many of those who survive this disaster, then turn to God and give Him glory.

Even though the passage in Revelation 11 ends with…

Rev. 11:14 - The second woe is past; [and], behold, the third woe cometh quickly.

This is not referring to the work of the Two Great Witnesses. It is referring to the slaughter by the 200,000,000 man army in Rev. 9:13-21. It is simply saying this as an introduction to the Third Woe, which is coming as the Seventh Trumpet Judgment.

The Third Woe (which is also the Seventh Trumpet) covers the last half of the Tribulation. So, it will be covered in Lesson 5. But there are some other events in the first half of the Tribulation that must be mentioned here.

There will be two great human institutions that will be working throughout the first half of the Tribulation. Space does not allow us to have a lengthy discussion of these, but a brief explanation will suffice at this point.

1. **The Revived Roman Empire**

We know from our earlier study, that Antichrist will come to power AFTER the Rapture, but prior to the start of the Tribulation. His rise to power will involve the overthrow of three of the ten kings who rule over the Revived Roman Empire (Dan. 7:8). But as stated earlier, he will replace those three and rule over the ten kings who will be his subordinates.

So, for the duration of the first half of the Tribulation (the first 3 ½ years), the greatest national power on earth will be the Revived Roman Empire, headed by Antichrist and his ten regional kings. And, as we've already discussed, Antichrist will be going out "conquering and to conquer" (Rev. 6:2), expanding his empire. This will be the cause of much of the warfare and bloodshed during the first half of the Tribulation.

2.   The One World Religion (Ecclesiastical Babylon)

From BEFORE the time of the Rapture and right into the first half of the Tribulation, there will be a "hierarchy of religion"… a kind of "United Nations of Religion" that will be in charge of ALL the religions of the world. Its goal will not be to convert all people into one doctrinal belief, but to promote cooperation and tolerance for the sake of "world peace". At some point (probably still during the Church Age), mankind will argue that most of the world's wars have happened as a result of religious belief. So, to prevent this, an over-arching ruling authority will be established to supervise all religions.

In the process, this authority will become very wealthy and powerful. Rev. 17 pictures the one-world religious system as a very wealthy woman riding on the back of the beast (Antichrist) which means that she (it) will have power and authority over the Antichrist until the mid-point of the Tribulation when the whole system will be destroyed by the ten kings who desire her wealth (Rev. 17:16). But for the first half of the Tribulation, the World Religions System will be very powerful and wealthy and a persecutor of all true believers who refuse to bow to its authority.

It is clear that even the first half of the Tribulation (which will not be as painful as the second half) will be a time of great warfare, bloodshed, and destruction. No part of Daniels' Seventieth Week will be without great heartache. And no one in his right mind should want to experience it. And today, the Good News is that you don't have to!

By trusting Jesus Christ as your personal Savior now (before the Rapture), you can know that you will be removed from this world before the whole planet starts "coming apart at the seems".

If you have not yet sought the salvation of Jesus, do NOT delay. The Rapture could happen at any moment and you would be left behind to face the worst time in all of human history!

The First Half of the Tribulation

Lesson 3 Quiz

1.   T or F It is not possible to understand the book of Revelation.

2.   Near the end of Daniel's book, God tells the prophet in Dan. 12:9 to "Go thy way, Daniel: for the words are closed up and sealed" until when?

3.   And the next verse says, "…and none of the wicked shall understand, but the _____ shall understand."

4.   And yet, at the end of the book of Revelation, God tells John in Rev. 22:10, "Seal not the sayings of the prophecy of this book: for [what?]"

5.   Although the book of Revelation is written basically in chronological order, there are within it some _____ passages.

6.   Rev. 4:1 - After this I looked, and, behold, a door was opened in heaven: and the first voice which I heard was as it were of a trumpet talking with me; which said,
_____ _____ _____ , and I will shew thee things which must be hereafter.

7.   When John is called up to Heaven in Rev. 4:1, it is symbolic of what?

8.   There are a total of [how many?] judgments of God in Revelation. And they are divided into what three groups?

9.   The first four Seal Judgments are often called what?

10.   For those who die for their faith in Christ Jesus, there is a special reward in Heaven for them called The _____ Crown (Rev. 2:8-11).

The First Half of the Tribulation

Lesson 3 Quiz Answers

1. FALSE. God gave it to us to "reveal" some things about the future.

2. Until the time of the end.

3. wise

4. for the time is at hand

5. Interval

6. Come up hither

7. The Rapture of the Church

8. 21, 7 Seal Judgments, 7 Trumpet Judgments, 7 Bowl Judgments

9. The Four Horsemen of the Apocalypse

10. Martyr's

What Happens After the Rapture?

Lesson 4
The Middle of the Tribulation

It is necessary that we discuss the events that will transpire in the "middle" of the Tribulation because the Bible reveals many things that will happen at that time. But when we say the "middle", we should not confine ourselves to the EXACT mid-point of the sevens year, but to that general time (of perhaps several weeks) around the exact middle.

The Bible is very specific (as we've already discussed) that the Tribulation (aka Daniel's Seventieth Week) will last for seven years of 360 days each (see Dan. 9:24-27, Rev. 12:6, 14, 13:5), or 2520 days. With that in mind, we would probably agree that there is a specific SECOND that falls exactly at the mid-point of the seven years. So, when we speak of events that happen at the middle of the Tribulation, we are NOT suggesting that all these events happen simultaneously at that very second. It is much more sensible to recognize that the "middle of the Tribulation" events will happen around that general time frame, within perhaps a few days or weeks before or after the exact to-the-second mid-point.

In our last lesson, we skipped over Rev. 10, which is an "interval" passage that reveals some things to us about what is about to happen.

At this point, six of the seven Trumpet Judgments (and the first two of three "Woes") have been completed. And, just as the breaking of the seventh seal contained the seven Trumpet Judgments, the seventh Trumpet Judgment coming up at this point will contain the seven Bowl Judgments (which is the Third Woe) which will complete the 21 Judgments of God that will be poured out on this earth during the seven year Tribulation.

The Mighty Angel and the Little Book

For a short time during the Middle of the Tribulation, there is a suspension of Judgments after the completion of the Sixth Trumpet Judgment and before the commencement of the Seventh Trumpet Judgment and the final Seven Bowl Judgments.

During that time, John saw a "mighty angel" descend to earth from Heaven and stand with his right foot on upon the sea and his left foot on the dry land. In his hand, he held an open "little book".

Rev. 10:1 - And I saw another mighty angel come down from heaven, clothed with a cloud: and a rainbow *was* upon his head, and his face *was* as it were the sun, and his feet as pillars of fire:

2   And he had in his hand a little book open: and he set his right foot upon the sea, and *his* left *foot* on the earth,

From the description given of the "mighty angel" in verse one, and comparing it to the description of our Lord Jesus Christ in Rev. 1, we must conclude that the "mighty angel" is in fact, Jesus Christ. In Scripture, it is not unheard of for Jesus to be referred to as an angel (see Ex. 3:2-18).

The book in the Lord's hand is NOT the same as the seven sealed book of chapter five, which judgments at this time are still being completed since the seventh seal contains the seven Trumpets and the seventh trumpet contains the seven Bowl Judgments. This "little book" is fully open, meaning its contents are revealed.

Rev. 10:5 - And the angel which I saw stand upon the sea and upon the earth lifted up his hand to heaven,

6   And sware by him that liveth for ever and ever, who created heaven, and the things that therein are, and the earth, and the things that therein are, and the sea, and the things which are therein, that there should be time no longer:

At this point, Jesus lifts His hand up toward Heaven and swears "there should be time no longer", or literally, that there should be no more delay. This means that the final seven plagues are now going to be poured out on earth… and the most horrific time in all of history is about to begin.

The contents of the mysterious little book are now revealed as the things which the seventh trumpet will cause to happen.

Rev. 10:7 - But in the days of the voice of the seventh angel, when he shall begin to sound, the mystery of God should be finished, as he hath declared to his servants the prophets.

John is told by Jesus to take the little book and eat it. When he did, he found it to be sweet to the taste, but it made his stomach bitter. He is then told…

Rev. 10:11 - And he said unto me, Thou must prophesy again before many peoples, and nations, and tongues, and kings.

Perhaps the sweetness was the knowledge that he would yet speak the prophetic message of God, but when he realized how awful that message was, it was bitter for him.

We now pick up where we left off in chapter 11 after the story of the Two Great Witnesses with the blowing of …

The Seventh Trumpet (the Third Woe)

Rev. 11:15 - And the seventh angel sounded; and there were great voices in heaven, saying, The kingdoms of this world are become *the kingdoms* of our Lord, and of his Christ; and he shall reign for ever and ever.

With the blowing of the Seventh Trumpet, the announcement is proclaimed in Heaven that Christ is now about to take back what rightfully belongs to Him… "the kingdoms of the world", which He won on the day of His resurrection. Even though we understand that there are still 3 ½ years of judgments coming, after which Christ will return to destroy His enemies and take His place on His throne in Jerusalem, this proclamation initiates "the beginning of the end" for the enemies of Christ.

The Sun-Clad Woman – An "Overview Interval" in Rev. 12

The twelfth chapter of Revelation is another "interval passage" that breaks with the chronological sequence in the book. It is neither a "flash forward" nor a "flash back", but BOTH. It is a break in the middle of the book to give a brief OVERVIEW of the entire story of Christ's redemptive work and Satan's persecution of the Jewish people as a result of their part in that redemptive plan. Although the story is presented in symbolic language, behind that symbolism is a literal story that a good student of the Word can easily recognize. I might also add that it is a fascinating story that reveals some important events of the Tribulation.

The passage begins with a description of woman in heaven.

Rev. 12:1 - And there appeared a great wonder in heaven; a woman clothed with the sun, and the moon under her feet, and upon her head a crown of twelve stars:

And she being with child cried, travailing in birth, and pained to be delivered.

The word translated as "wonder" is the Greek word "semeion" which carries the meaning of a "sign, miracle, wonder, or token". So, in actuality, what John sees is symbolic and is a **sign** pointing to literal historical events, some of them already past and some still futuristic, as we will see.

But WHO is this woman? Some would say that she represents the church because we will read that she births the Christ child. But the Church did not give birth to the Christ. Christ gave birth to the Church!

As with all symbols, the best approach to interpreting them is to see how they are used elsewhere in the Bible. In this case, all three symbols of the "sun, moon, and stars" are used in Gen. 37:9. There, Joseph describes a dream that he had where the sun, moon, and eleven stars all bowed down to him. The next verse makes it clear that the sun represented Joseph's father, Jacob. The moon represented his mother, Rachel. And the eleven stars represented his eleven brothers. All together, we recognize these 13 people and Joseph as the beginning of the people of Israel… the Jewish people.

It is FROM the Jewish people that Jesus came. So, without a doubt the sun-clad woman represents the Jewish people.

By her description (clothed with the sun, moon under her feet, etc.), we immediately recognize that this woman is not a certain human, but represents a greater entity than just a single human being. As we said, that entity is the Jewish people.

Rev. 12:3 - And there appeared another wonder in heaven; and behold a great red dragon, having seven heads and ten horns, and seven crowns upon his heads.

4   And his tail drew the third part of the stars of heaven, and did cast them to the earth: and the dragon stood before the woman which was ready to be delivered, for to devour her child as soon as it was born.

The seven-headed, ten-horned, red dragon who is ready to "devour her child as soon as it was born" is later identified for us in verse 9 when he is cast out of heaven:

Rev. 12:9 - And the great dragon was cast out, that old serpent, called the Devil, and Satan, which deceiveth the whole world: he was cast out into the earth, and his angels were cast out with him.

So, the red dragon is Satan. And, you will remember the story of how Herod the Great killed the baby boys in Bethlehem in an attempt to kill Jesus, the One whom the wise men from the East had come to worship (Matt. 2). Even though Herod saw baby Jesus as a future threat to his throne, there is no doubt that Satan was behind this horrible massacre, trying to kill the "child as soon as it was born".

The "third part of the stars of heaven" refers to the one third of God's angels who were thrown out of Heaven at the time of Satan's rebellion. Although we don't know the exact number of these fallen angels, their numbers must be huge. They are still serving Satan today and will one day face a particular judgment for their actions (Jude 1:6).

The child birthed by the sun-clad woman is clearly identified as Jesus in the next verse.

Rev. 12:5 - And she brought forth a man child, who was to rule all nations with a rod of iron: and her child was caught up unto God, and *to* his throne.

After the birth and later, the ascension of Jesus to Heaven where He now sits on His throne, the story makes a giant leap forward in time to the last half of the Tribulation… the last 1260 days.

Rev. 12:6 - And the woman fled into the wilderness, where she hath a place prepared of God, that they should feed her there a thousand two hundred *and* threescore days.

This fleeing into a God-prepared place in the wilderness by the Jewish people will happen at the middle of the Tribulation. Later in the chapter, we will read that they are fleeing from the persecution of Satan through his man, the Antichrist.

The Abomination of Desolation

Jesus warned in His Olivet Discourse that when they see the "Abomination of Desolation spoken of by Daniel the prophet", that they should immediately run for their lives.

Matt. 24:15 - When ye therefore shall see the abomination of desolation, spoken of by Daniel the prophet, stand in the holy place, (whoso readeth, let him understand:)

16   Then let them which be in Judaea flee into the mountains:

But, what is the "Abomination of Desolation"? Daniel 9:27 tells us that at the mid-point of the Tribulation, Antichrist will break his seven-year covenant (peace treaty) with Israel. He will then move into Jerusalem and take control of it. In his super egotistical pride, he then sits in the Temple and there proclaims to the whole world that he is God (probably the Messiah that the Jews have been waiting on, the Mahdi that the Muslims have been waiting on, and the Savior that the Christians have been waiting on… all wrapped up in one).

Paul says that he…

2 Thess. 2:4 - …opposeth and exalteth himself above all that is called God, or that is worshipped; so that he as God sitteth in the temple of God, shewing himself that he is God.

This act of the Antichrist when he desecrates the Temple of God in Jerusalem and makes his blasphemous claim to divinity is the "Abomination of Desolation".

At that time, Antichrist will start an unprecedented persecution of the Jews, trying to kill every last one. That's why Jesus told them to run for their lives.

Matt. 24:15 - When ye therefore shall see the abomination of desolation, spoken of by Daniel the prophet, stand in the holy place, (whoso readeth, let him understand:)

16   Then let them which be in Judaea flee into the mountains:

17   Let him which is on the housetop not come down to take any thing out of his house:

18   Neither let him which is in the field return back to take his clothes.

[skipping to verse 21]

21   For then shall be great tribulation, such as was not since the beginning of the world to this time, no, nor ever shall be.

22   And except those days should be shortened, there should no flesh be saved: but for the elect's sake those days shall be shortened.

Jesus said for them to flee into the "mountains". John said the woman will take refuge in the "wilderness". Most scholars believe that this place where God will supernaturally protect and care for this fleeing remnant of Jews is in the southern part of the modern nation of Jordan… probably in the area of Petra because of its naturally fortified situation in the mountains.

So, the "fleeing of the remnant of Jews from the persecution of Antichrist" will happen in the middle of the Tribulation and God will protect them in a specially prepared place in the wilderness for the last half of the Tribulation.

Now, before we read the next two verses, which talk about Satan, let's jump to the next chapter and read about…

The Antichrist

Rev. 13 describes two "beasts" that John sees. The first one (the more prominent one) has seven heads and ten horns just like the red dragon (Satan) in chapter 12. However, this beast is not Satan. It is a symbol of Antichrist and his kingdom. And we read in 13:3…

Rev. 13:3 - And I saw one of his heads as it were wounded to death; and his deadly wound was healed: and all the world wondered after the beast.

4   And they worshipped the dragon which gave power unto the beast: and they worshipped the beast, saying, Who *is* like unto the beast? who is able to make war with him?

We don't have time to go into a full discussion of the seven heads and ten horns. But what I want you to see here is an event that will happen in the middle of the Tribulation.

Many scholars believe that where verse 3 says, "And I saw one of his heads as it were wounded to death" refers to an apparent death blow to Antichrist (probably an assassination attempt) where he will appear to have been killed. But then, miraculously, he comes back to life (probably three days later) in a counterfeit of the resurrection of Jesus.

There are also some who believe the deadly wound to just one of the seven heads speaks of the revival of the Antichrist empire from the old Roman Empire. But this does not explain why people respond the way they do in verse 4. There, it says that they are amazed and say, "Who is like unto the beast? Who is able to make war with him?" It appears that they are so amazed by this miraculous recovery from the deadly wound that they say these things about the MAN Antichrist and begin to worship both Antichrist and Satan (which is what both of them want).

Here's the point…
At the time of the deadly wound is received by Antichrist, Satan will literally embody and possess him, taking full control of him for the remainder of the Tribulation.

Even though we have read of many horrible events that will happen in the first half of the Tribulation, there is no doubt that the last half of the Tribulation will be far worse. That's why Jesus said that AFTER the Abomination of Desolation (at the mid-point), "then shall be GREAT Tribulation…" (Matt. 24:21). It is in the last half that Satan will be confined to earth, having been kicked out of Heaven. (Back to Rev. 12)

Rev. 12:7 - And there was war in heaven: Michael and his angels fought against the dragon; and the dragon fought and his angels,

8   And prevailed not; neither was their place found any more in heaven.

At the time of Satan's original rebellion in the timeless past, he lost his position as the great archangel of God and was relegated to living on earth (Ezek. 28:12-19, Isa. 14:6-15) and to moving about in its atmosphere as the "prince of the power of the air" (Eph. 2:2). However, he did not lose his access to the throne room of God where he still works as the "accuser of the brethren" (Rev. 12:10) for we read that he approached the Lord in Heaven to accuse Job (Job 1:6).

But here, we are reading about another "war in heaven" during the Tribulation where Michael (the archangel of God) and his angels will fight against Satan and his angels. The result will be that Satan and his angels will be thrown out of heaven (that is, lose access to heaven) and confined to earth. Because, after this "neither was their place found any more in heaven." And this greatly angers Satan!

9   And the great dragon was cast out, that old serpent, called the Devil, and Satan, which deceiveth the whole world: he was cast out into the earth, and his angels were cast out with him.

10   And I heard a loud voice saying in heaven, Now is come salvation, and strength, and the kingdom of our God, and the power of his Christ: for the accuser of our brethren is cast down, which accused them before our God day and night.

11   And they overcame him by the blood of the Lamb, and by the word of their testimony; and they loved not their lives unto the death.

12   Therefore rejoice, ye heavens, and ye that dwell in them. [There is rejoicing in Heaven when Satan is no longer allowed to enter there.] Woe to the inhabiters of the earth and of the sea! for the devil is come down unto you, having great wrath, because he knoweth that he hath but a short time.

The prophet Isaiah also spoke of this future war (Isa. 26:20, 27:1).

Once Satan is cast out of heaven, he enters into Antichrist and begins his persecution of the Jews.

The rest of Rev. 12 makes clear that Satan will pursue the fleeing Jews with the armies of Antichrist, but this all happens in the last half of the Tribulation. And since we are trying to describe events in a somewhat chronological order, we will not cover the rest of this chapter at this time.

The False Prophet and the Mark of the Beast

The second beast mentioned in Rev. 13 is symbolic of a man who is the top official under the rule of Antichrist. We call him the False Prophet because that is what he is called elsewhere in the book of Revelation (Rev. 16:13, 19:20, 20:10). We have discussed him in earlier lessons, but since we're looking at Rev. 13 where he is described, let's take another look at this insidious person.

Rev. 13:11 - And I beheld another beast coming up out of the earth; and he had two horns like a lamb, and he spake as a dragon.

The first beast is said to come up out of the sea which is always a reference in Bible Prophecy to the Gentile nations of the world (see Dan. 7:3). But this second beast comes up "out of the earth" which is a reference to the land of Israel. For this (and other reasons), I believe that the False Prophet will be a Jew from Israel.

Again, in prophetic symbolism, a "horn" (like a horn on the head of a cow) is always symbolic of a person of power, like a king or general (Dan. 7:24). A horn can also represent one's power, which is the case in this verse. Because this beast has two small lamb-like horns, it indicates that he does not possess great power… at least, not at first. But, his appearance is misleading because he speaks like a dragon which refers to the great power in his speech, particularly because it has satanic power. Repeatedly, as we've already seen in Rev. 12, Satan is portrayed as a dragon.

As the "False Prophet", his goal is to cause the inhabitants of Earth to worship the Antichrist.

Rev. 13:12 - And he exerciseth all the power of the first beast before him, and causeth the earth and them which dwell therein to worship the first beast, whose deadly wound was healed.

Just as the Holy Spirit is the third person of the Holy Trinity (Father, Son, and Holy Spirit), the False Prophet is the third person of the Unholy Trinity (Satan, Antichrist, and False Prophet). And just as the Holy Spirit works to point people to Jesus, the False Prophet will work to point people to Antichrist.

Not only does the False Prophet have satanically inspired speech, he is also endowed with certain supernatural powers by Satan as well.

Rev. 13:13 - And he doeth great wonders, so that he maketh fire come down from heaven on the earth in the sight of men.

14a   And deceiveth them that dwell on the earth by the means of those miracles which he had power to do in the sight of the beast...

Using his persuasive speech and supernatural powers, he has a statue of Antichrist built and placed in the Temple and gives it the life-like ability to speak. Then, he requires all people to worship the statue (image) under the penalty of death.

Rev. 13:14b - ...saying to them that dwell on the earth, that they should make an image to the beast, which had the wound by a sword and did live.

15   And he had power to give life unto the image of the beast, that the image of the beast should both speak, and cause that as many as would not worship the image of the beast should be killed.

Not only is the False Prophet the world religious leader, he also heads up the finances of the Antichrist Empire. Using his control of the world's financial infrastructure, he forces all people to receive a mark on their right hand or forehead to show their loyalty to Antichrist and his empire. It is a mark that serves two purposes.

1. It is a visible mark of loyalty. So, those who do not have it can be identified as subversives of the empire and can be prosecuted (or executed). In some way, it will be acceptable for each person to have either this mark, or the name of Antichrist, or the number 666 which will be the numerical value of the name of Antichrist. Having at least one of these will allow a person to buy and sell.

2. It is used to make sales transactions. Just as we would use a credit card, or debit card today, it will be "swiped" to identify the person it is on as the owner of the associated bank account. All sales transactions, both private and public, will be made using this mark on one's body. So, if a person does not have it, he cannot buy or sell anything, making it very difficult to obtain food and other necessities.

Rev. 13:16 - And he causeth all, both small and great, rich and poor, free and bond, to receive a mark in their right hand, or in their foreheads:

17   And that no man might buy or sell save he that had the mark, or the name of the beast, or the number of his name.

18   Here is wisdom. Let him that hath understanding count the number of the beast; for it is the number of a man, and his number is six hundred threescore and six. **[666]**

Today, we've grown accustom to making our purchases without the transfer of any paper money (cash or check). Totally digital sales transactions are used daily by almost everyone. Soon, the arguments will be made that to reduce card fraud, to prevent accidental loss of cards, and to insure accurate personal identification of the one making the purchase, the BEST way will be to put your ID number on your body.

Sub dermal microchips have already been developed that can be used to identify and TRACK a person, no matter where he is on the planet. These invisible chips under the skin can also be used in the same way a debit card is used. A quick scan of the right hand or forehead and "Transaction Complete!" This is not futuristic sci-fi! This technology is here now.

The personal privacy watchdogs will oppose forcing people to have a unique personal ID number on their body until… a serious terrorist attack similar to that of 9/11/01 happens. Then, when the federal government says that the only way that they can protect us from such terrorism is for every person to have a personal ID number, people will gladly comply. Later, when Antichrist is on the scene, he will use this system that will already be operational to implement his "mark of the beast" program.

In recent years, banking systems around the world have become interconnected through the use of satellite communications. Today, it is easy to withdraw funds from your local bank account even when you're visiting some country on the other side of the world. So, the worldwide computer systems infrastructure is already in place to handle every sales transaction on the planet.

So, the systems and technology are now in place that Antichrist will use one day to implement his "Mark of the Beast" program.

Fall of the "United Nations of Religion"

In Rev. 17, John describes the unusual sight of a magnificently wealthy harlot riding on the back of the beast with seven heads and ten horns [the Antichrist and his kingdom]. She sips leisurely from a golden chalice filled with all kinds of abominations and the blood of the saints and the martyrs of Jesus.

Rev. 17:6a - And I saw the woman drunken with the blood of the saints, and with the blood of the martyrs of Jesus...

This woman is symbolic of a worldwide authority over all religions that will be established to regulate and control all religions around the planet. I refer to it as the "United Nations of Religion" (UNR). We already explained how that in the first half of the Tribulation, this entity will become very powerful and wealthy under the leadership of the False Prophet. But, somewhere around the middle of the Tribulation, the ten regional kings under the Antichrist will overthrow and destroy the UNR and steal her wealth. As a show of loyalty and to obtain the blessings of Antichrist, they will then insist that all people worship ONLY the Antichrist. THIS will be the final one-world religion.

Rev. 17:12 - And the ten horns which thou sawest are ten kings, which have received no kingdom as yet; but receive power as kings one hour with the beast.

13   These have one mind, and shall give their power and strength unto the beast.

[skipping down to verse 16]

16   And the ten horns which thou sawest upon the beast, these shall hate the whore [the UNR], and shall make her desolate and naked, and shall eat her flesh, and burn her with fire.

17   For God hath put in their hearts to fulfill his will, and to agree, and give their kingdom unto the beast, until the words of God shall be fulfilled.

So, in summary of this lesson about the events that will happen in the middle of the Tribulation, we have…

1. The Antichrist breaks the seven-year covenant with Israel and moves into Jerusalem, taking full control of the city and all of Israel.
2. The False Prophet orders a statue of the Antichrist to be built and put in the Temple. And then, he orders all people to bow down and worship it.

3. While televised and broadcast around the world, Antichrist sits in the Temple and claims to be God… the "savior" that the world has been waiting for.
4. The False Prophet implements the "Mark of the Beast" program demanding that all people must take the mark of loyalty to the Antichrist. Without it, a person will not be allowed to buy or sell anything.
5. An assassination attempt is made on the Antichrist with a sword in which he appears to die.
6. Satan is cast down to earth and enters into the body of Antichrist making it appear that he has been resurrected from the dead.
7. In his boiling rage against the Jews, Satan (through Antichrist) begins to try to kill all Jews, beginning in Judea.
8. A remnant of Jews escape the persecution of Antichrist by running into the wilderness in southern Jordon where they find a place of protection where Antichrist's armies cannot get to them.
9. In his rage, Antichrist kills the two Great Witnesses whose bodies lie in the streets of Jerusalem for 3 ½ days. Then, suddenly they are resurrected and fly away into the sky to Heaven.
10. In a conspiracy, the ten kings under the rule of Antichrist destroy the United Nations of Religion and steal its wealth. And in a show of loyalty, demand that all people must worship ONLY the Antichrist.

It is difficult to say what the exact order of these events will be, but it is with some confidence that we can say they all happen in the general time frame of the "Middle of the Tribulation".

God forbid, but if you should reject the salvation of Jesus Christ now, before the Rapture, and find yourself trying to survive through the seven years of Tribulation, AT ALL COST… EVEN THE COST OF YOUR LIFE… DO NOT ACCEPT THE ANTICHRIST! DO NOT WORSHIP HIM OR HIS IMAGE! AND MOST IMPORTANTLY, DO NOT TAKE HIS MARK!

Rev. 14:9 - And the third angel followed them, saying with a loud voice, If any man worship the beast and his image, and receive *his* mark in his forehead, or in his hand,

10   The same shall drink of the wine of the wrath of God, which is poured out without mixture into the cup of his indignation; and he shall be tormented with fire and brimstone in the presence of the holy angels, and in the presence of the Lamb:

11   And the smoke of their torment ascendeth up for ever and ever: and they have no rest day nor night, who worship the beast and his image, and whosoever receiveth the mark of his name.

The Middle of the Tribulation

Lesson 4 Quiz

1.   The "mighty angel" in Rev. 10 is a reference to who?

2.   In Rev. 12, the "sun-clad woman" is symbolic of who?

3.   In Rev. 12, the "Red Dragon" is symbolic of who?

4.   T or F   Today (in the Church Age), Satan is confined to earth and cannot enter Heaven.

5.   When Antichrist sits in the Temple in Jerusalem and claims to be God, this horrific sin is called what?

6.   And this event happens in what part of the Tribulation?

7.   In Rev. 13:3-4, the Antichrist will appear to duplicate what act of Jesus Christ?

8.   According to Rev. 13, what two significant acts of the False Prophet will he do to give honor and glory to the Antichrist?

9.   According to Revelation 17, who conspires together to destroy the "United Nations of Religion" (my name for it)?

10.   If a person is not saved when the Rapture occurs, and gets left behind to try to live in the Tribulation, can he still be saved?

The Middle of the Tribulation

Lesson 4 Quiz Answers

1.   Jesus

2.   the Jewish people

3.   Satan

4.   False. As the Accuser of the Brethren, he still has access to the throne room of God.

5.   The Abomination of Desolation

6.   the mid-point

7.   The death and resurrection

8.   (1) He will put an image of the Antichrist in the Temple and require people to worship it.
    (2) He will require all people to take a mark of loyalty to the Antichrist.

9.   The ten kings

10.   Yes. But it will be very difficult as he will probably have to die for his faith.

What Happens After the Rapture?

Lesson 5
The Last Half of the Tribulation

After the many events that happen in the middle of the Tribulation, the earth will enter into what some scholars call The GREAT Tribulation… the last half (3 ½ years) of the seven-year Tribulation that will culminate with the glorious Second Coming of Jesus Christ. The last half is sometimes distinguished from the first 3 ½ years or the WHOLE seven years as the GREAT Tribulation period for two reasons. (1) Jesus referred to the last half as a time of GREAT Tribulation (Matt. 24:21), and (2) Even though the first half of the Tribulation will be filled with horrible judgments from God, warfare, and persecutions, the LAST HALF (3 ½ years) will be the time of the Third Woe… the seven BOWL judgments, which will be even worse than the first 14 judgments (Seal and Trumpet judgments) of the first half!

One might ask, "How could things get any WORSE than what we've already read about in the first half and middle of the Tribulation?" Well, just listen as we now enter into our study of THE GREAT TRIBULATION!

We begin this lesson with another "interval passage" that discusses a heavenly event.

Rev. 14:1 - And I looked, and, lo, a Lamb stood on the mount Zion, and with him an hundred forty *and* four thousand, having his Father's name written in their foreheads.

Here, "Mount Zion" is NOT the earthly Mt. Zion in Jerusalem, but the heavenly Mt. Zion… the same one that is referred to in…

Heb. 12:22 - But ye are come unto mount Zion, and unto the city of the living God, the heavenly Jerusalem, and to an innumerable company of angels,

Jesus is standing on the heavenly Mt. Zion and with Him are the 144,000 sealed servants of God that we read about in chapter 7 when they were chosen and sealed by God to minister in the first half of the Tribulation. But since we now see them in Heaven, we must assume that they were all martyred or translated bodily to heaven by this time.

Rev. 7:3 told us that they were "sealed in their foreheads". And here, we come to understand what that seal actually is. It is "his Father's name", that is, the name of the father of The Lamb of God. So, the seal is actually the name of our Heavenly Father!

In ancient times, a "seal" upon something indicated ownership. In the case of these special 144,000 servants of God, we are to understand that they are CHOSEN by God for His special purpose (preaching the Gospel of the Kingdom to all the nations of the world, Matt. 24:14), for a special time (the first half of the Tribulation). So, God protects them from the Antichrist until they have completed their task and then He brings them home where we see them playing music and singing a special song that only they knew.

Rev. 14:2 - And I heard a voice from heaven, as the voice of many waters, and as the voice of a great thunder **[the voice of the Lamb of God]**: and I heard the voice of harpers harping with their harps:

3   And they sung as it were a new song before the throne, and before the four beasts, and the elders: and no man could learn that song but the hundred *and* forty *and* four thousand, which were redeemed from the earth.

Another outstanding characteristic of these special servants is that they are all **virgin men**. This is especially significant when one considers that the most prevalent and overwhelming sin of the Tribulation (even in the first half) will be sexual immorality and perversion. As Paul told Timothy that "in the latter times some shall… forbid[ding] to marry." This is NOT a reference celibacy, but is a statement that men will no longer see a need for "traditional marriage", or for that fact, any kind of marriage as society is enveloped in open sexual relationships.

Rev. 14:4 - These are they which were not defiled with women; for they are virgins. These are they which follow the Lamb whithersoever he goeth. These were redeemed from among men, *being* the firstfruits unto God and to the Lamb.

Next, John sees three angels flying through the atmosphere of planet earth, one after the other, proclaiming three messages to the world below. Because of the extreme importance of these three messages, God uses this supernatural means of delivering them to the human race so that NO ONE can say that they didn't know about them.

Angel No. 1 - Proclaims the "everlasting gospel" and says, "Fear God, and give glory unto Him; for the hour of his judgment is come: and worship Him that made heaven, and earth, and the sea, and the fountains of waters." (Rev. 14:7)

Nowhere else in all of Scripture do we find where God uses an angel to declare His gospel message to the people of earth. But here, God will do this to ensure that every living soul on the planet will hear His "everlasting gospel" which is the proclamation of coming judgment... "for the hour of his judgment is come".

Since the word "gospel" means "good news", how can the message of God's coming judgment be good news? It will be good news to those who are being persecuted by the Antichrist that SOON their troubles will be over... because the Creator God, Jesus Christ, is coming to judge His enemies on earth and the time of the redemption of those being persecuted is at hand.

Angel No. 2 - Flies through the atmosphere announcing that "Babylon is fallen, is fallen, that great city, because she made all nations drink of the wine of the wrath of her fornication."

This is the announcement of the destruction of the literal city of Babylon, which will become the international headquarters of Antichrist during the Tribulation. We will talk more about God's destruction of Babylon later when we get to chapter 18.

Angel No. 3 - Follows the first two, declaring that anyone who takes the mark of the beast is doomed forever.

Rev. 14:9 - And the third angel followed them, saying with a loud voice, If any man worship the beast and his image, and receive *his* mark in his forehead, or in his hand,

10   The same shall drink of the wine of the wrath of God, which is poured out without mixture into the cup of his indignation; and he shall be tormented with fire and brimstone in the presence of the holy angels, and in the presence of the Lamb:

11   And the smoke of their torment ascendeth up for ever and ever: and they have no rest day nor night, who worship the beast and his image, and whosoever receiveth the mark of his name.

Rev. 14:14-20 gives us "flash-forward" to the time of the Lord's Second Coming, which will happen at the end of the Tribulation. In an analogy of reaping a harvest of grapes with a sickle, Jesus (the One who sits upon a white cloud with a crown upon His head and a sickle in His hand) reaps the harvest of those souls from earth who belong to Him.

Then, an angel does the same thing except that his harvest is the souls of those who reject Jesus. They are thrown into "the great winepress of the wrath of God" and when they are squashed, "blood came out of the winepress, even unto the horse bridles, by the space of a thousand and six hundred furlongs" [about 200 miles]. This is a description of the enormity of the bloodshed in and around Israel at the time Jesus defeats His enemies at His Second Coming.

Beginning in chapter 15, John sees a great host of the Tribulation Martyrs who had remained faithful unto the Lord, standing on an immense pavement that is like glass with fire flashing in it. And they sang "the song of Moses" and "the song of the Lamb", which brings great honor and glory to the Lord.

Starting in Revelation 16, we have the pouring out of the seven Bowl Judgments, which are "full of the wrath of God" (Rev. 15:7). The suffering that is caused by these judgments is beyond our comprehension! This will be the pinnacle... the absolute climax of all God's punishment on earth against all those millions of people who hate Him and rejected His Son. Nothing in all of human history can even come close to the pain and suffering that will be inflicted by these seven judgments.

By the time this happens in the last half of the Tribulation, most all the people who will be saved during the Tribulation will have already been saved under the preaching of the special 144,000 special servants of God in the first 3 ½ years. And even though most of those will have already died as martyrs (Rev. 6:9-11, 7:9-17,15:2-4), there will be some who will have managed to stay alive into the last half. It is of them particularly that Jesus spoke when He said,

Matt. 24:13 - But he that shall endure unto the end, the same shall be saved. [in both a spiritual and physical sense]

Bowl Judgment No. 1 - Grievous Sores

Rev. 16:1 - And I heard a great voice out of the temple saying to the seven angels, Go your ways, and pour out the vials [or, bowls] of **the wrath of God** upon the earth.

2 · And the first went, and poured out his vial upon the earth; and there fell a noisome and grievous sore upon the men which had the mark of the beast, and *upon* them which worshipped his image.

Something akin to the worst possible case of leprosy will afflict the followers of Antichrist... those who had taken his mark. Grotesque, oozing, infectious, open wounds that continually agitate the nerves, sending constant pain throughout the body will be their judgment. But since it befalls them "which had the mark of the beast", we may assume that those who had NOT taken the mark and had managed to live to this point in time, will be spared from this excruciating torture.

Bowl Judgment No. 2 - Death to the Sea Creatures

Rev. 16:3 - And the second angel poured out his vial upon the sea; and it became as the blood of a dead *man*: and every living soul died in the sea.

The second Bowl Judgment causes the immediate pollution of the sea as it turns a brownish red and stinks like the rotting blood of a dead man. And all over the world, the beaches are filled with the stench of tons of rotting flesh as the dead and bloated sea creatures are washed ashore. As far as the eye can see across the horizons of the ocean, there is a plane of dead, floating sea creatures of every sort.

Bowl Judgment No. 3 - Polluting of the Fresh Water Sources

Rev. 16:4 - And the third angel poured out his vial upon the rivers and fountains of waters; and they became blood.

Following the poisoning of the oceans, the fresh water sources on earth (rivers and springs) suddenly become red and polluted so that nothing can live in them and the water is unfit for drinking.

As we read of these horrible things, it certainly hurts our sensibilities. We are shocked by the thought of such gruesome judgments and may question ourselves as to WHY a God of love could do such things. But I remind you that God is not only a God of LOVE, but one of perfect justice. Every soul that suffers these unimaginable things, will DESERVE what they get.

Rev. 16:5 - And I heard the angel of the waters say, Thou art righteous, O Lord, which art, and wast, and shalt be, because thou hast judged thus.

6   For they have shed the blood of saints and prophets, and thou hast given them blood to drink; for they are worthy.

7   And I heard another out of the altar say, Even so, Lord God Almighty, true and righteous *are* thy judgments.

Some may wonder how they can be happy in Heaven, knowing that their lost loved ones are suffering unbelievable torment in Hell. This mindset shows great spiritual immaturity and a total lack of understanding concerning the life hereafter. Once we are in that glorified state in the presence of our blessed Savior… once we have begun to literally FEEL His glory and love, we will be so totally in love with Him… so completely engrossed in His unbelievable grace for loving us undeserving creatures, that we will, like the angels in these verses, declare that His judgments are TRUE AND RIGHTEOUS. And that all those who rejected His great love, DESERVE all that they getting.

Bowl Judgment No. 4 - Scorching Heat

Rev. 16:8 - And the fourth angel poured out his vial upon the sun; and power was given unto him to scorch men with fire.

9   And men were scorched with great heat, and blasphemed the name of God, which hath power over these plagues: and they repented not to give him glory.

In these last horrible days of the age, God will cause the brightness and heat of the sun to dramatically increase. As God did in the days of Moses when He sent plague after plague upon the Egyptians that showed His superiority over all the things that the Egyptians worshipped, once again those who love the sun and love to feel its rays warming their naked skin… and, for those who perhaps even WORSHIP the sun (which is just one of trillions of stars that God created), God will use that great body to torment them with unquenchable heat. It will be impossible to go outdoors unprotected from the sun's rays because of the burning heat. Air conditioning systems will overheat and melt down, leaving people to swelter inside in unyielding heat.

And yet, in all of that agonizing pain… "they repented not to give him glory". Such hardness of the human heart cannot be understood. But sin, given enough time, can take the most pure and innocent little baby, and bring him to the point of such cursing hatred of God. It's just a matter of time for leaven once introduced in the loaf will spread until it consumes the whole loaf. And sin, even in the heart of an innocent babe, without the intervention of God in that person's life, will continue to spread and eat away at him till he too becomes that hardened, blaspheming hater of God.

And the people in this time of the Tribulation, instead of repenting of their sins and crying out to God for forgiveness, will bow their necks and shake their fist at God, screaming that He cannot break them. But they have no idea what still awaits them…

Bowl Judgment No. 5 - Darkness

Rev. 16:10 - And the fifth angel poured out his vial upon the seat of the beast; and his kingdom was full of darkness; and they gnawed their tongues for pain,

11   And blasphemed the God of heaven because of their pains and their sores, and repented not of their deeds.

In the midst of the putrefying sores, the stench of rotting flesh, and the insufferable heat, God turns out all the lights. For a time there is no natural or man-made light that can pierce the intensely thick darkness. It is impenetrable by even man-made light. Staggering about like blind men, people will be forced to simply "sit and soak" in their agonizing pain.

Nothing scares people like the unknown. And nothing creates so much unknown as being enveloped in total darkness. Everything around us… even the things of which we are completely familiar, suddenly become the "unknown". This situation will create unbearable terror in the hearts of humans. Even a few hours of it will cause people to lose their minds in fear. Screaming and cursing will not bring relief. And so they blaspheme God with every ungodly and vulgar language imaginable. But it changes nothing.

In what was once the beautiful land of Israel, there has been years of war and bloodshed. Most all of the Jews have fled Jerusalem and the surrounding area (Judea) to escape the persecution of the Antichrist. It is now overrun with Muslim Arabs and other Gentiles.

Here, we turn to the prophet Daniel's writings about

The Willful King - Antichrist

Dan. 11:36 - And the king [Antichrist] shall do according to his will; and he shall exalt himself, and magnify himself above every god, and shall speak marvellous things against the God of gods, and shall prosper till the indignation [the Tribulation] be accomplished: for that that is determined shall be done.

In Daniel 9:24, God tells Daniel what He has determined to do to Daniel's people, the Jews.

Dan. 9:24 - Seventy weeks *are determined* upon thy people and upon thy holy city, to finish the transgression, and to make an end of sins, and to make reconciliation for iniquity, and to bring in everlasting righteousness, and to seal up the vision and prophecy, and to anoint the most Holy.

In the time in which we are living today (2015) in the Church Age, all but the last "week" of years that God said He had determined to deal with Daniel's people has happened. The first 69 "weeks" of years ended at the time of the Crucifixion. At that time, God "stopped His clock" of the seventy years of dealing with Daniel's people and turned His attention to the Gentile nations of the world to gather out unto Himself a very special, blood-washed multitude called THE CHURCH.

But when the Church has been fully "built"… when the last person to be saved in the Church Age is saved and the Bride of Christ is complete, the GROOM (Jesus Christ) will come for His Bride in that great event that we call the RAPTURE of the Church.

THEN, God will turn His attention BACK to Daniel's people to finish the Seventieth Week of Daniel… or, what we call, The Tribulation. THIS has been DETERMINED by God and it WILL BE DONE!

Now, back to what Daniel says Antichrist will do near the end of the Tribulation.

Dan. 11:40 - And at the time of the end shall the king of the south [south of Israel, which would be Egypt] push at him [make some aggressive moves at him]: and the king of the north [this is a reference to Antichrist who at that time will be just north of Israel] shall come against him [the king of the south… Egypt] like a whirlwind, with chariots, and with horsemen, and with many ships; and he shall enter into the countries, and shall overflow and pass over. [He will take control of Egypt and even some neighboring countries (maybe Sudan and Libya).]

41   He shall enter also into the glorious land [pass through Israel], and many *countries* shall be overthrown: but these shall escape out of his hand, *even* Edom, and Moab, and the chief of the children of Ammon. [Edom, Moab, and Ammon are all in the modern nation of Jordan. Why will Antichrist bypass Jordan? Because, you will remember that God will be protecting the remnant of Jews who fled from Jerusalem into Jordan.]

42   He shall stretch forth his hand also upon the countries: and the land of Egypt shall not escape.

43   But he shall have power over the treasures of gold and of silver, and over all the precious things of Egypt: and the Libyans and the Ethiopians *shall be* at his steps [will be subservient to him].

Now, here is the important part to our study…

44   But tidings out of the east and out of the north shall trouble him: therefore he shall go forth with great fury to destroy, and utterly to make away many.

In the midst of his campaign to subdue Egypt and the north African countries, Antichrist will suddenly get some disturbing news about something "out of the east and out of the north" , probably that the far eastern nations are rebelling against him and have mobilized their armies and are moving into the Middle East to confront him. So, he will move out of north Africa back into the land of Israel.

45   And he shall plant the tabernacles of his palace between the seas in the glorious holy mountain; yet he shall come to his end, and none shall help him.

"Between the seas" is between the Dead Sea and the Mediterranean Sea and "the glorious holy mountain" is a reference to Jerusalem (which is between the Dead and the Med. Seas).

Now, let's go on with our study of the Bowl Judgments in the book of Revelation.

Bowl Judgment No. 6 - Preparing the Way for the Kings of the East

As we approach the final days of the Tribulation in our study, preparation is made for bringing hundreds of millions of soldiers from "the east" (perhaps China, Indonesia, India, and others) into the land around Israel, by drying up the Euphrates River.

Rev. 16:12 - And the sixth angel poured out his vial upon the great river Euphrates; and the water thereof was dried up, that the way of the kings of the east might be prepared.

And then the unholy Trinity spews forth three filthy demonic spirits that have the appearance of horrible, slimy, grotesque frog-like creatures. They go forth into the world and work miracles through those who are unknowingly the tools of Satan to convince the leaders of the nations to rebel against Antichrist, who at that time is in Israel.

13   And I saw three unclean spirits like frogs *come* out of the mouth of the dragon, and out of the mouth of the beast, and out of the mouth of the false prophet.

14   For they are the spirits of devils, working miracles, *which* go forth unto the kings of the earth and of the whole world, to gather them to the battle of that great day of God Almighty.

[skipping to verse 16]

16   And he gathered them together into a place called in the Hebrew tongue Armageddon.

This gathering together of the nations will cover a large part of the Middle East. A major staging area will be the Valley of Jezreel in northern Israel (also known as the Valley of Armageddon in the Bible) for the Scripture says "he gathered them together" there. But remember from Daniel that Antichrist will be set up in Jerusalem, probably with most of his armies to the west toward the Mediterranean and to the south toward Egypt. So, the main part of the war between Antichrist and the armies that have come from the east and from the north will be around Jerusalem (Zech. 14:1-9).

Somewhere along about this time, God will destroy the great city of Babylon which will be the headquarters of Antichrist and both a religious and commercial center for the whole world. It could be that this is the troubling news he hears about in the east which angers him so, because Babylon is on the Euphrates River about fifty miles south of Baghdad and about 850 miles east of Jerusalem.

The Bible doesn't make it clear as to exactly how Babylon is destroyed other than it being a judgment of God. However, Rev. 18:15 tells us that her merchants stood far away "for the fear of her torment" (radiation?) and Rev. 18:8 says, "she shall be utterly burned with fire" and Rev. 18:18 says that the merchants "cried when they saw the smoke of her burning" (a nuclear mushroom cloud?). So, it is certainly possible that the rebelling nations advancing from the east could destroy Babylon with a nuclear explosion.

Nevertheless, with the Euphrates River dried up and the stronghold of Babylon out of the way, the eastern armies advance right to the land of Israel to confront Antichrist.

Then, the seventh and final Bowl Judgment is poured out.

Rev. 16:17 - And the seventh angel poured out his vial into the air; and there came a great voice out of the temple of heaven, from the throne, saying, It is done.

The proclamation that "It is done" means that it is finished. The judgments of God have come to an end with this last Bowl Judgment, but it is really a BIG judgment.

Rev. 16:18 - And there were voices, and thunders, and lightnings; and there was a great earthquake, such as was not since men were upon the earth, so mighty an earthquake, *and* so great.

19   And the great city was divided into three parts, and the cities of the nations fell: and great Babylon came in remembrance before God, to give unto her the cup of the wine of the fierceness of his wrath.

20   And every island fled away, and the mountains were not found.

21   And there fell upon men a great hail out of heaven, *every stone* about the weight of a talent: and men blasphemed God because of the plague of the hail; for the plague thereof was exceeding great.

In the midst of the mother of all earthquakes, hundred pound hail stones pulverize the earth! And the result? Did men repent and turn to God? No! They blasphemed God!

Then, at this climactic moment when hundred of thousands of soldiers have gathered around Jerusalem and the earth is shaken by the greatest earthquake ever, and some areas are pulverized by giant hail stones...

JESUS, THE KING OF KINGS AND LORD OF LORDS, BURSTS THROUGH THE ATMOSPHERE AND WITH THE SWORD OF HIS MOUTH, HE DESTROYS THE ARMIES OF ANTICHRIST AND THE OTHER NATIONS!

Rev. 19:11 - And I saw heaven opened, and behold a white horse; and he that sat upon him *was* called Faithful and True, and in righteousness he doth judge and make war.

12   His eyes *were* as a flame of fire, and on his head *were* many crowns; and he had a name written, that no man knew, but he himself.

13   And he *was* clothed with a vesture dipped in blood: and his name is called The Word of God.

14   And the armies [which were] in heaven followed him upon white horses, clothed in fine linen, white and clean.

15   And out of his mouth goeth a sharp sword, that with it he should smite the nations: and he shall rule them with a rod of iron: and he treadeth the winepress of the fierceness and wrath of Almighty God.

16   And he hath on *his* vesture and on his thigh a name written, KING OF KINGS, AND LORD OF LORDS.

[skipping down to verse 19]

19   And I saw the beast, and the kings of the earth, and their armies, gathered together to make war against him that sat on the horse, and against his army.

20   And the beast was taken, and with him the false prophet that wrought miracles before him, with which he deceived them that had received the mark of the beast, and them that worshipped his image. These both were cast alive into a lake of fire burning with brimstone.

21   And the remnant were slain with the sword of him that sat upon the horse, which *sword* proceeded out of his mouth: and all the fowls were filled with their flesh.

No matter how hard we may try... It is impossible for us to comprehend the devastation, pain, and bloodshed of the Tribulation. That's why Jesus said,

Matt. 24:21 - For then shall be great tribulation, such as was not since the beginning of the world to this time, no, nor ever shall be.

22   And except those days should be shortened, there should no flesh be saved: but for the elect's sake those days shall be shortened.

If Jesus did not return at that specific time, man would destroy himself completely from the face of the earth. In fact, I am sure in those last days, many people will believe that the end of humanity on earth had come.

It will be a time of Hell on Earth! Hell will have a holiday and Satan will almost accomplish his goal of destroying all of mankind.

But the Good News today is that you don't have to go through all of that. Today... NOW, while we're still in this wonderful Age of Grace, each of us has the wonderful privilege of being able to ask Jesus to forgive us our sins and save us. Then, as a new born again believer in Jesus Christ, He will remove us from this earth before the Tribulation begins.

If it should turn out that you die the physical death before the Rapture happens, then the Lord will immediately escort you to that Sweet Beulah Land... that place where "eye hath not seen, nor ear heard, neither have entered into the heart of man, the things whicth God has prepared for them that love Him." (1 Cor. 2:9)

It is that place called Heaven. It is a real place and you can spend eternity there in the presence of Jesus Christ... But "ye must be born again"! (John 3:7)

The Last Half of the Tribulation

Lesson 5 Quiz

1.   The last half of the Tribulation is often referred to as what?

2.   The 144,000 special servants of God are sealed in their forehead with what name?

3.   T or F   The 144,000 special servants of God will live on earth until the end of the Tribulation.

4.   In the last half of the Tribulation, God will use how many angels to fly through the air and proclaim His messages to the inhabitants of earth?

5.   T or F   Any person who takes the mark of the beast can still be saved if they repent and turn to God.

6.   The seventh Trumpet Judgment contains the seven Bowl Judgments and this is called the Third _____.

7.   According to Rev. 16:5, after Bowl Judgment No. 3 when the fresh water sources are polluted, the "angel of the waters" proclaims what?

8.   According to Rev. 16:16, God gathers the armies of the nations into a valley called what?

9.   The white horse rider in Rev. 19 who is called "Faithful and True" is who?

10.   And this is a description of Him at what event?

The Last Half of the Tribulation

Lesson 5 Quiz Answers

1. The Great Tribulation

2. The name of God the Father

3. False. We see that they are in Heaven in Rev. 14 in the last half of the Tribulation.

4. Three

5. False (see Rev. 14:9-11)

6. Woe

7. That God's judgments are righteous.

8. Armageddon

9. Jesus

10. The Second Coming